SUFFOLK'S MILITARY HERITAGE

Adam Culling

AMBERLEY

Front cover top: Crew of the USAAF 388th Bombardment Group, 'Little Boy Blue'. Flying from RAF Knettishall, the B-17 was involved in a mid-air collision on 19 July 1944 and crashed in Thurston. (National Archives, D.C.)

Front cover bottom: The unique quatrefoil-shaped Martello tower near Aldeburgh, now owned by The Landmark Trust, which allows the tower to be used as a holiday home.

Back cover: Replica Blue Danube bomb near the entrance to the Gorse Industrial Estate.

First published 2026

Amberley Publishing
The Hill, Stroud
Gloucestershire, GL5 4EP

www.amberley-books.com

ISBN 978 1 3981 2589 6 (print)
ISBN 978 1 3981 2590 2 (ebook)

British Library Cataloguing in Publication Data.
A catalogue record for this book is available from the British Library.

Origination by Amberley Publishing.
Printed in Great Britain.

Appointed GPSR EU Representative: Easy Access System Europe Oü, 16879218
Address: Mustamäe tee 50, 10621, Tallinn, Estonia
Contact Details: gpsr.requests@easproject.com, +358 40 500 3575

Contents

Introduction

The county of Suffolk has a prominent and varied cultural heritage. Its residents have made significant contributions to the arts such as Benjamin Britten, the composer and conductor whose best-known works include *War Requiem*, who was born in Lowestoft and later made Aldeburgh his home. The world-renowned artist Thomas Gainsborough, whose paintings can be found in The National Gallery, Victoria and Albert Museum, and the Ashmolean Museum (to name but a few), hailed from the small market town of Sudbury. The county is home to one of the most significant archaeological discoveries pertaining to Anglo-Saxon culture, with the excavations of the Sutton Hoo burial mounds in the mid-twentieth century. Yet its military heritage is equally varied and also holds regional and national importance; it combines the physical reminders of centuries of conflicts with the modern role that the county plays in ensuring foreign and domestic security.

The county has some 60 miles of shoreline and approximately 1,400 square miles of rural and urban landscape, so it is near impossible to not stumble upon its physical reminders of war. This poses the dilemma as to which conflicts associated with the county of Suffolk to include: the county has been associated with conflict for over two millennia and so it would be impossible to mention all of those who were affected by such events, and the impact the conflicts have had locally, nationally, and potentially internationally. As with all historical research, the survival of documents – and indeed the availability of those that did – has played a role in the selection of locations represented in the book. While an attempt has been made to include a range of villages, towns and cities from across Suffolk, some areas will be more underrepresented than others. While this is not to diminish the importance of these unmentioned military events, it is simply that others have either piqued my interest, or that I would consider the failure not to include those that I have to be a greater crime. I hope you enjoy this journey through Suffolk's military past and that it inspires you to discover more both about the county's fascinating landscape and the remarkable lives of those that represent Suffolk's Military Heritage.

Suffolk's Early Military Heritage

Suffolk is blessed with an abundance of archaeological material. The towns and villages across Suffolk offer evidence of bronze and iron age settlements, with recovered objects displayed in local history, major partnership and national museums. The excavations carried out at Sutton Hoo in 1938 by Basil Brown, and the subsequent discovery of the Saxon burial ship and the objects that were recovered the following year, provide a unique insight into Anglo-Saxon traditions and culture. However, Suffolk's earliest large-scale and organised military heritage was the Roman occupation of Britain. In fact, one of the defining military events between the Roman occupants and native Britons originates in Suffolk: the assault on the Iceni tribe leader's family and the retribution against their attackers that ensued.

The physical reminders of Roman occupation in Suffolk remain today. Archaeological evidence provides us with a map of where Romans villages and villas were situated, and of course the pioneering road networks that Roman engineers created. However, the survival of Roman military structures in the county is rather scarce. Even in the neighbouring counties of Essex and Norfolk the only significant Roman structures that were associated with protection or other military functions that have survived are the Roman walls that were incorporated into the defences of Colchester, the Saxon Shore forts at Burgh Castle in Norfolk and Bradwell-on-Sea in Essex. This later example of Roman military architecture is also associated with some of Suffolk's earliest military heritage, despite its location being somewhat inaccessible (for most people). The Saxon Shore forts were built by the Roman Empire during the third and early fourth century. Constructed to several different plans, they offer an insight into the development of Roman military architecture for the period. It is believed that they were built in response to early Saxon raiders, having been built along the coast at points where penetration into the Roman provinces was likely. Their name derives from the late fourth-century document the 'Notitia Dignitatum' – the Register of Dignitaries– where the control of the nine Roman forts came under the 'Comes Litoris Saxonici' – the Count of the Saxon Shore. The Saxon Shore forts protected the coastline of the Roman provenances in Briton, stretching from Portchester in Hampshire to the northern part of the Norfolk coastline.

Despite its relative inaccessibility, in 1969 a team of divers from the Ipswich branch of the British Sub-Aqua Club, led by Jeff Errington, examined the ruins of Walton Castle – a Saxon Shore fort submerged off the Felixstowe coast. The expedition was reported in the *East Anglian Daily Times* in December 1969, and recounted how the local divers found two of the walls of the Roman fort, which extended from the remains of a corner bastion. One wall ran for 90 yards almost parallel with the shore; the other ran 40 yards out to sea and measured 9 feet thick and between 4 and 5 feet tall. They noted that the concrete mortar was as hard as the stones themselves – a testament to Roman engineering. Pieces of the

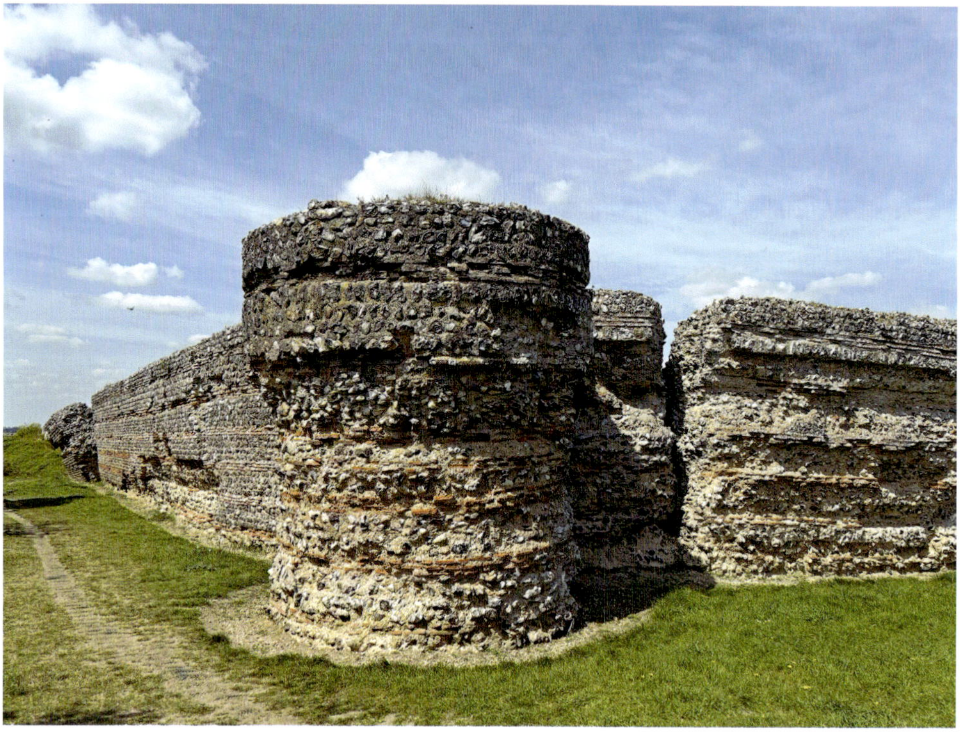

Walton Castle had a similar design to that of Burgh Castle (pictured) in Norfolk.

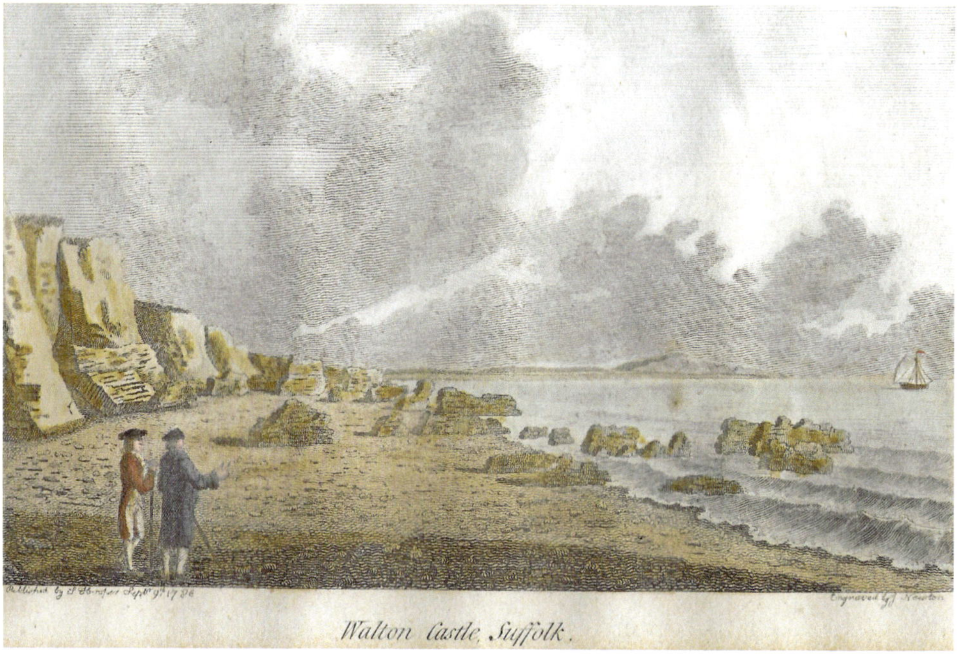

A late eighteenth-century print showing the ruins of Walton Castle being taken by the sea.

wall were recovered and documented by Elizabeth Owles, the Ipswich Museum liaison, and now forms part of their collection. Walton Castle would continue to be utilised after the Romans departed in the fifth century, with the Normans building a keep inside its walls, until it began to be dismantled by Henry II in 1174 as a reprisal for Hugh Bigod's part in the Revolt of 1173–74. Walton Castle was still in use in 1338, when Edward III lodged there before sailing to France for the Crecy campaign. It would be 1,400 years after it was constructed that the advancing sea would finish Henry's destructive work.

While the Saxon Shore forts were used to defend against Saxon raiders, it would be the local inhabitants that would cause the first and only potentially devastating challenge to Roman rule. Early in the Roman occupation of Britain, the Celtic tribes that offered no opposition to Roman conquest were afforded certain privileges. The Iceni tribe, whose territory included what is now parts of modern-day Suffolk and Norfolk, were one of these pro-Roman tribes. By accepting Roman occupation, they would become a 'client kingdom'. For the Romans, this ensured they kept the peace in their domain, saving them the expense of needing to garrison the area, while the Iceni benefitted from the support of Romans against any potential rivals. When the Iceni king, Prasutagus, died in AD 60 without a male heir, the Romans nullified their agreement with the Iceni, despite Prasutagus naming his wife, Boudicca, his successor. The Roman commanders refused to recognise women to be the Iceni kings' heirs. When Boudicca failed to accept this, she and her daughters were assaulted, providing the catalyst for Boudicca and the Iceni to revolt against the Romans. The Iceni incited the Trinovantes and other tribes to join them in

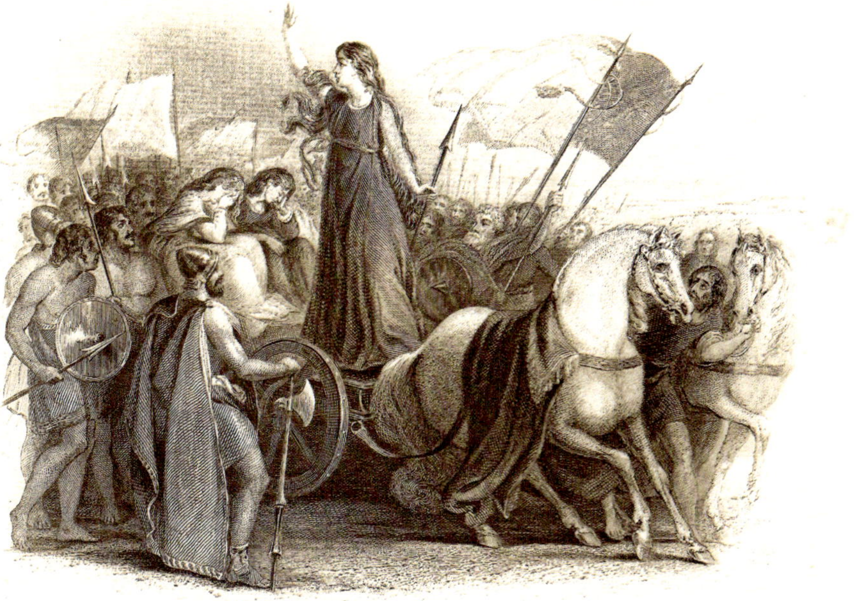

Boudicca rallying her people against the Romans.

their rebellion, and the first target of their combined force was the relatively unprotected Camulodunum, modern-day Colchester. Following their sacking of Colchester, Boudicca and her forces continued to amass support as they travelled towards St Albans and London, the new administrative centre of Roman Britain. Prior to arriving in London, Boudicca's forces clashed with a large detachment of the Roman IX Legion near modern-day Haverhill. While the exact location is unknown, it is believed the soldiers of the IX were defeated near the village of Great Wratting.

Following the Roman departure from Britain during the fifth century, the country would become home to the Anglo-Saxons. Having travelled from present-day Germany, Denmark and Holland, the Angles settled in *Ēastengla* – the kingdom of the East Angles, now known as East Anglia, which incorporates modern-day Suffolk. While skirmishes and battles took place between the kingdom of the East Angles and the neighbouring kingdom of Mercia, which resulted in the deaths of several East Anglian kings, it would be Viking raiders in the ninth century that would ultimately lead to the kingdom's demise. In AD 865 'The Great Heathen Army' – a full-scale Viking invasion force – arrived on Suffolk's shores. Viking attacks on Suffolk's coastal region began decades before, with Gypeswic's (more commonly known today as Ipswich) position in the estuary of the Orwell making it equally suitable for trading and a target of Viking raiders. As the Norsemen's ships travelled up the Orwell and Stour to attack inland settlements, the king of the East Angles – the boy King Edmund – made a deal with them. He acknowledged that his own forces could not match the Vikings', so allowed the Danes free passage and provided them with horses in return for them not attacking his land. The treaty allowed the Danes to over-winter at Thetford, across the Ouse and the modern-day border with Norfolk, before attacking Mercia and Northumbria the following spring. Within a couple of years, the Vikings had returned to their camp at Thetford, and – disregarding their treaty with King Edmund – began attacking settlements and Christian monasteries in East Anglia. It wouldn't be until AD 869 that King Edmund's and the Viking invaders' forces would face each other in a fierce battle that would result in the death of the King of the East Angles. When King Edmund's army succumbed to the brutal attacks by the Danes, Edmund was captured and tortured by the Vikings who demanded he renounce his Christian faith. When Edmund refused, he was tied to a tree and struck with numerous arrows before being decapitated. Some accounts recall that this took place near Hoxne. What followed has become part of King Edmund's legend: when the king's men searched for his body, they had trouble locating his head. When the king's men heard the cry of 'here, here, here' from a nearby wood, they discovered a wolf protecting Edmund's head. It is said that when the wolf allowed the men to retrieve the head and place it with the king's body, it miraculously reattached. Edmund's remains were moved to Bedricsworth, modern-day Bury St Edmunds, where King Athelstan established a religious community to care for a shrine that would become a place of national pilgrimage. The Danish king, and later King of England, Cnut, who had converted to Christianity before he was king of England, built a stone Abbey on the site of the Shrine in AD 1020. Ipswich would continue to be a target for the Vikings, and would be occupied by the Scandinavians from AD 869 until AD 917, when the town was recaptured by Anglo-Saxon forces. It wouldn't be too long before the Vikings returned to Ipswich: in AD 991 the Vikings, under the command

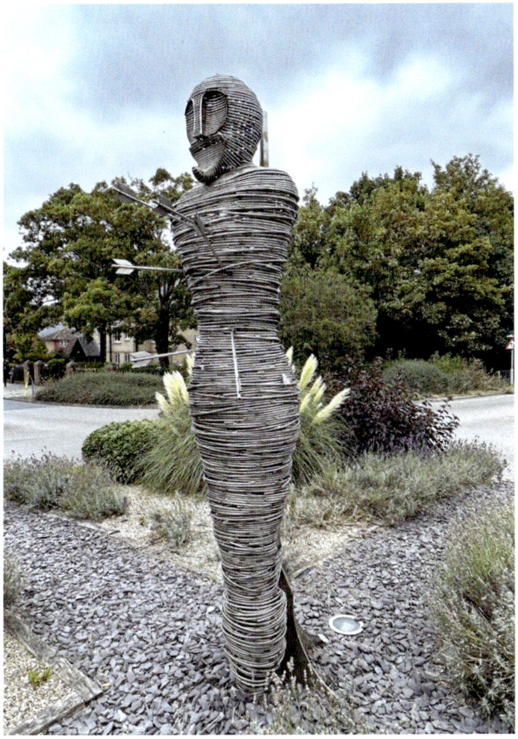

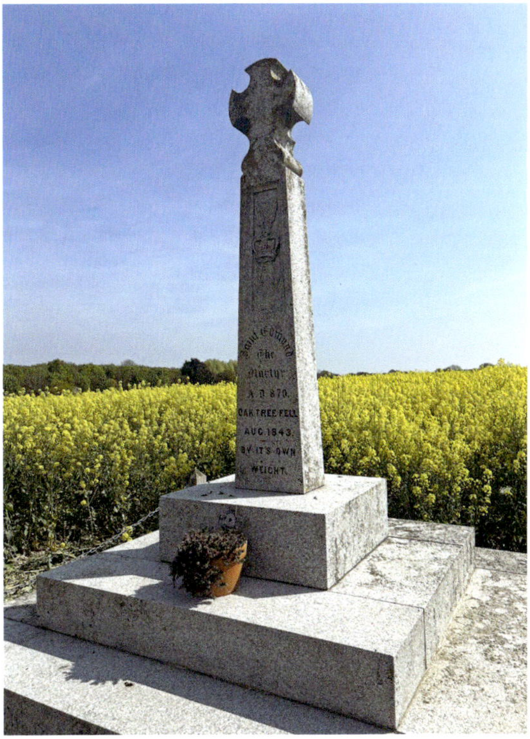

Above left: A sculpture at Bury St Edmunds' Parkway-Risbygate roundabout, depicting King Edmund having been struck by arrows when he refused to renounce his Christian faith.

Above right: King Edmund's Memorial Cross at Hoxne, believed to be the site of Edmund's death at the hands of the Vikings.

Bottom right: A wooden wolf statue in Bury St Edmunds' Abbey Park. A reminder of the legend of King Edmund's decapitated head being recovered.

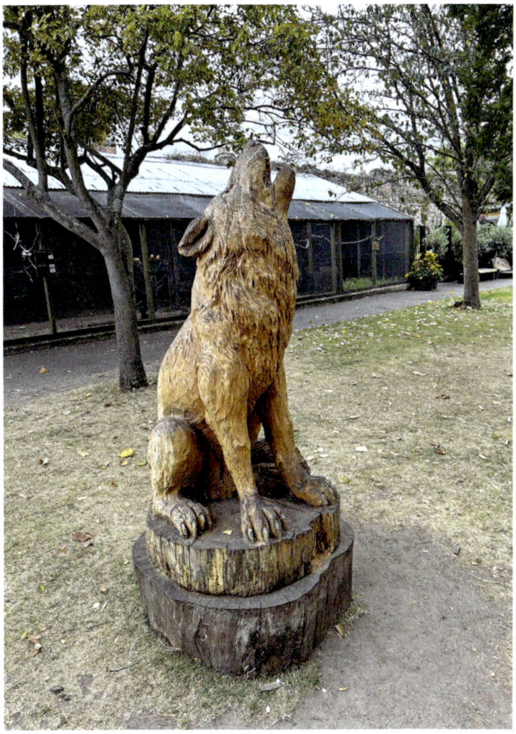

of the future King of Norway Olaf Tryggvason, amassed their forces there before travelling down the coast to the Blackwater estuary to meet the Anglo-Saxon army, led by Ealdorman Byrhtnoth, in the Battle of Maldon. Tryggvason's victory over Byrhtnoth would ultimately mark the beginning of the end of Anglo-Saxon rule in Britain.

The Norman invasion and subsequent conquest of England in 1066 would be the end of Anglo-Saxon and Viking control of Suffolk and East Anglia. While the invasion and the Battle of Hastings had very little impact on Suffolk, the enduring Norman influence on Suffolk's physical landscape is evident in the structures whose roots can be traced to the period. These castles, which will be discussed in more detail in the following chapters, would continue to be developed and adapted beyond the period of Norman rule, and would continue to play an important role in Suffolk's military past.

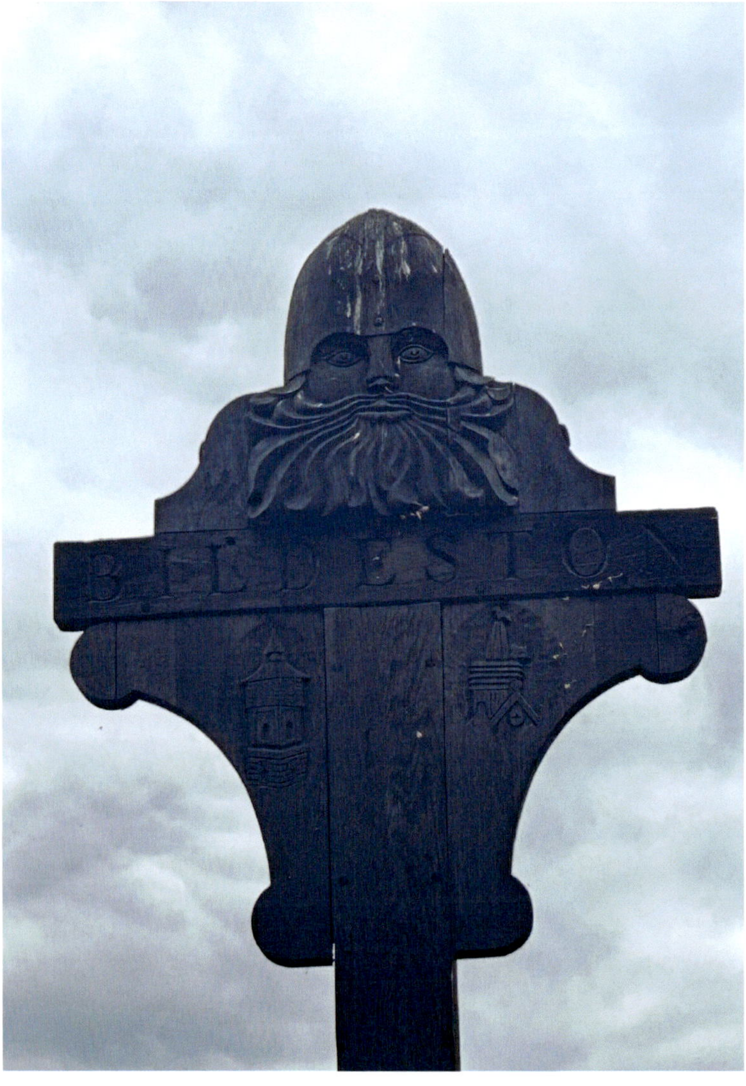

One of many towns and villages whose name has a Viking connection. Bildeston is an example of 'Grimston hybrid', combining the name of a prominent Viking, '*Bild*', and the Saxon word for estate or village, '*tun*'.

Rebellion and Destruction

The Norman invasion of England in 1066 offered a brief period of stability in Suffolk. The intermittent Viking attacks that plagued Ipswich between the seventh and early tenth centuries finally came to an end when Roger Bigod, a Norman knight who had travelled to England during the Norman conquest, held numerous lordships in Essex, Suffolk, and Norfolk. Under Bigod's protection, the Viking attack on Ipswich in 1069 was easily repelled, and with the realisation that Ipswich now had the means to protect itself, this became the final assault on Ipswich by Viking forces. The Norman period was, however, short-lived compared to the previous and subsequent ruling houses of England and Britain. This led to the years between the medieval and early modern England being a period of rebellion, reprisal, and ultimately destruction throughout Suffolk. Despite this, the unescapable legacy of the Norman conquest on Suffolk's landscape remains. Castles were a dominant feature of the Norman conquest, and while many of them have succumbed to the ravages of time, their design characteristics have endured for centuries as new fortifications fulfilled the role of their earlier counterparts: a symbol of power, protection and patronage. While in many cases very little of the ancient fortifications remain, it is evident that these castles were actively involved in the rebellions of the medieval period, destroyed for the part they played, or built in retaliation.

When Henry I's only legitimate son died onboard the *White Ship* in 1120, this caused an indivertible crisis upon Henry's death in 1135. A dispute over the succession of his daughter, Empress Matilda, resulted in civil war in England and Normandy because his nephew Stephen claimed the English throne. This era of unrest, and the accompanying breakdown in law and order, is often referred to as 'The Anarchy'. During this period, numerous castles were erected by barons as they vied to control land in East Anglia. The Bigod family, who had protected Ipswich from marauding Vikings, were not the saviours that many Anglo-Saxons may have hoped for. In 1074, Roger Bigod was appointed Sheriff of Norfolk and Suffolk and had a level of control over East Anglia that could arguably be considered similar to that of a local king. Roger was granted licences to build several castles in Norfolk and Suffolk which help consolidate the family's power. When Roger's son, William, also died on the *White Ship* without a legal heir his brother Hugh inherited his father's landholdings. Taking full advantage of these privileges, including using the castles at Framlingham and Bungay, he subdued the local Anglo-Saxon population and rebelled against the king. Hugh's openly rebellious actions against Henry II would ultimately lead to the confiscation of his castles at Framlingham, Bungay and Walton. In 1163 the king returned Framlingham and Bungay to Hugh Bigod, but retained Walton Castle in order to control the approaches by sea to the rebellious baron's stronghold at Framlingham. To further contain the influence of the troublesome baron, Henry II began constructing a royal castle at Orford in 1166, as a replacement for Walton Castle. Unlike Walton Castle, Orford survives substantially intact.

Despite King Henry II's best efforts to control the Bigods' influence in Suffolk, when his son, Henry the Young King, raised a rebellion against his father in 1173, Hugh Bigod saw an opportunity to restore his power and influence in the region: Hugh Bigod sided against King Henry II, having been promised Norwich Castle from Henry the Young King. While Henry II was fighting his son's forces in France, the Earl of Leicester, Robert Beaumont, took the opportunity to travel from Flanders to England with an army, mainly composed of Flemish mercenaries, and join with Hugh's forces. Upon landing his army at Walton in September 1173, the Earl of Leicester and Hugh attacked – but failed to sack – the still unfinished royal castle at Orford. Despite this setback, their rebel army was able to sack Haughley Castle, near Stowmarket. The rebel army returned to Bigod's castle at Framlingham, where they remained for a few days, when the Earl of Leicester decided to move his force closer to his own land around Leicester. Meanwhile, Richard de Lucy (Henry II's Justiciar) and Constable Humphrey de Bohun learned of Beaumont's plan while negotiating a truce in Scotland with William the Lion, and hurried to intercept the rebel army. Joining forces with the king's uncle Reginald, Earl of Cornwall, as well as Roger Bigod (Hugh's son), they confronted the rebel army near Bury St Edmunds. The two forces met on 17 October 1173, and what is now known as the Battle of Fornham started in Fornham St Martin and ended near Fornham St Geneive Church, along the River Lark's eastern side. The battle ended in a decisive victory for the Royalist army. After the battle, Hugh Bigod returned to the safety of his castle at Bungay, and after the king's forces had

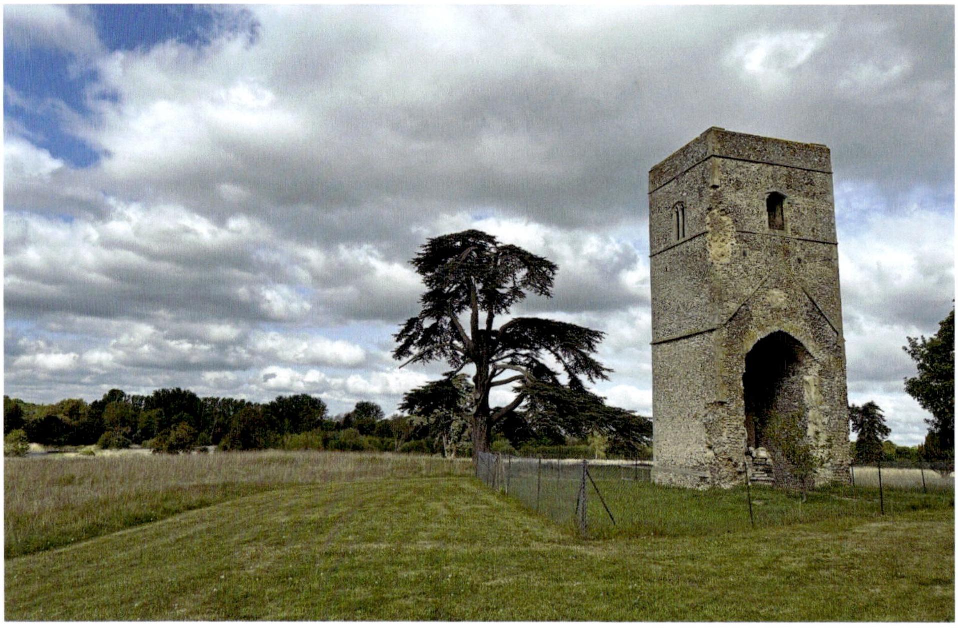

The site of the battle of Fornham, between the remains of the Church of St Genevive and the River Lark.

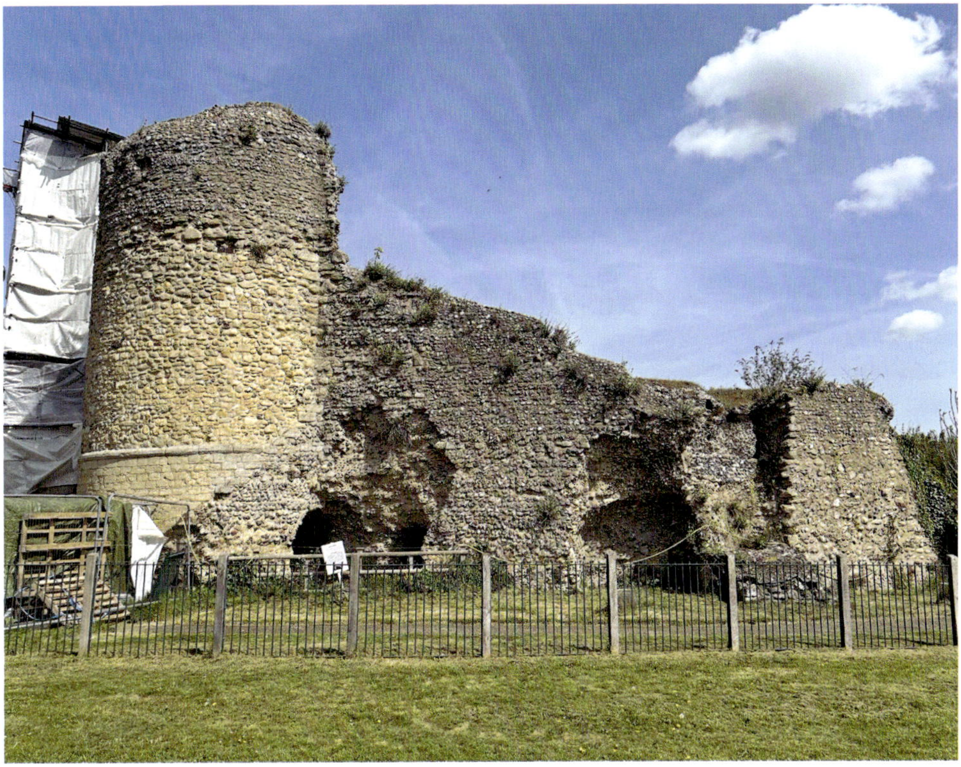

The ruins of Bungay Castle, currently under restoration.

marched to Framlingham and Bungay, he surrendered. The Revolt of 1173 had significant consequences on Suffolk's military landscape. Henry II ordered Walton Castle to be demolished, with only parts of the Roman fortifications surviving until it was finally lost to the North Sea. Hugh Bigod was forced to surrender his castles at Bungay and Framlingham; they would later be returned to the Bigod family until they reverted to the crown upon Roger Bigod's death in 1297. Framlingham Castle still dominates the town's high ground, while Bungay Castle's ruinous state remains an integral part of Suffolk's Norman heritage.

After Henry II's death, his three children would go on to rule England for the next fifty years. This period saw costly wars being waged abroad that would continue the Plantagenet family tradition of inciting rebellion against their barons. Many English barons were becoming increasingly frustrated with King John's lack of military and diplomatic competence, so twenty-five of them met at the Abbey of St Edmunds in late 1214. Here they set in motion the creation of the judicial document that would form the basis of English Law, and other countries' governing constitutions – the Magna Carta. Of these twenty-five barons who were committed to ensuring that the king abided by the provisions of this great charter, four were associated with Suffolk. True to form, the Bigod family were once again rebelling. Richard de Clare, 3rd Earl of Hartford and feudal baron of Clare, and his son Gilbert, whose family had built a motte-and-bailey castle in Clare soon after the Norman invasion, were also present. A year later, the same barons forced King John to sign the Magna Carta, limiting the king's power. This victory would be short-lived, for shortly after agreeing to the terms John declared war on the rebel barons. In late 1215, while King John was travelling to defeat those rebelling against him in the north, an army of French mercenaries led by Savari de Mauleon was tasked with quelling the rebellion in the east. In early March 1216, Royalist forces besieged Framlingham Castle, and despite having a garrison of twenty-six knights, serjeants and crossbowmen, the castle was surrendered after only two days. Framlingham and Bungay survived the rebellion and would be regranted to Roger Bigod following King John's death. In 1215, the rebel barons invited Prince Louis VIII of France to take the English throne. Louis' forces arrived in May 1216 and with the support of the barons, he had great success in capturing several Royalist castles, including Orford. When King John died of dysentery in October 1216, and his successor, Henry III, agreed to a revised charter, Louis' support from the barons waned and he was eventually forced to abandon his plans to become King of England.

Less than fifty years later, the English barons rebelled against their king once more. Unhappy with the country's financial situation and the prospect of another costly foreign war against the Hohenstaufen, a group of dissatisfied barons established the Provisions of Oxford in 1258. This sought to establish royal accountability to a council of barons – as

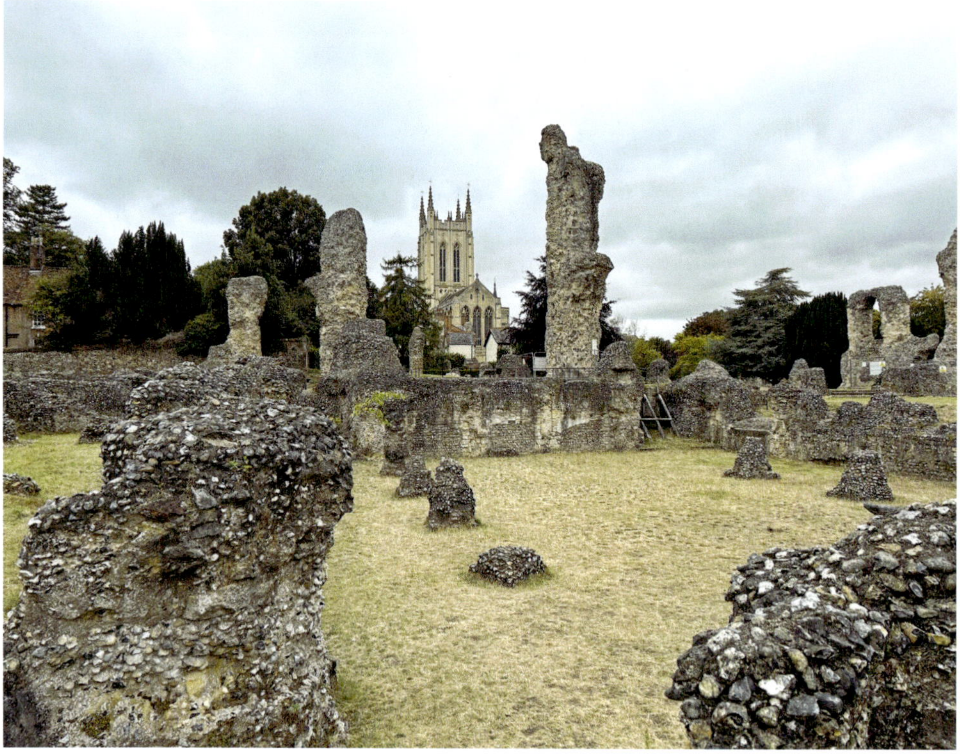

The site where the rebel barons met in 1214 at the Abbey in Bury St Edmunds.

opposed to a select few of the king's favourites – as a means of resolving disputes. As with the earlier Provisions with King John, Henry III reneged, which led to the Second Barons' War in 1264. Gilbert de Clare, like the Bigods of Suffolk, switched allegiances during this revolt. Despite de Montfort's military success in defeating King Henry III at the Battle of Lewes, and the establishment of the first English Parliament in early 1265, de Clare realigned with the monarchy, fighting with Henry III's son, Edward, at the Battle of Kenilworth in August 1265. Following the death of Simon de Montfort at the Battle of Evesham on 4 August 1265, successive rebel defeats led to the surrender of Kenilworth Castle in December 1266, and the creation of the Dictum of Kenilworth, annulling the rebel baron's Provisions of Oxford. Despite having helped draft the Dictum, in May 1267 de Clare seized London to force the king to amend it, allowing disinherited barons to recover their land before fines had to paid, thus easing the terms of surrender for rebellious barons.

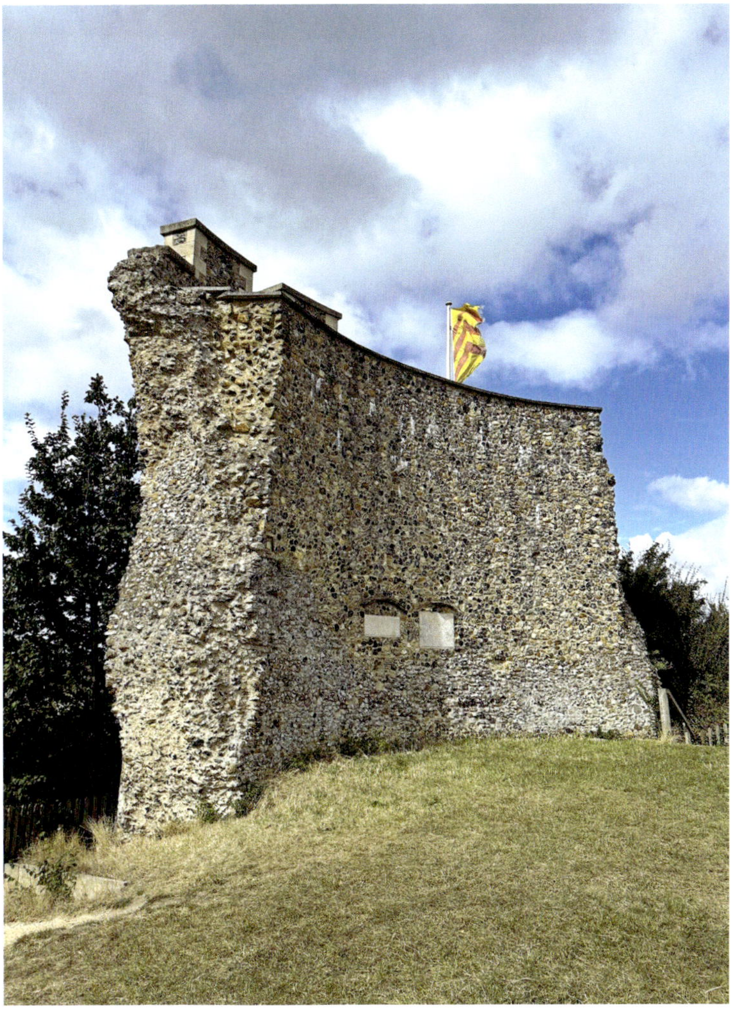

The ruins of Clare Castle, overlooking the grounds of Clare Castle Country Park.

Several castles in Suffolk were attacked during the Second Barons' War. Eye Castle, having been rebuilt after being sacked by the Bigods during the revolt of 1173, was again attacked in 1265, and – for the most part – abandoned thereafter. The royal castle at Orford, which had been given to Roger Bigod in 1261, was captured several times. Unlike in previous rebellions, the Bigods remained loyal to the king during the Second Barons' War. Despite King John having ordered Lidgate Castle to be destroyed for William de Hastings' dissention during the Barons' War of 1215, the castle survived and was inherited by William's son, Henry. Henry joined the rebel barons in 1264 and garrisoned the castle against the king. During the rebellion Henry was captured and repented to the king for his dissent, but ultimately rejoined the rebel barons before surrendering at the end of the conflict in 1267. The castle at Lidgate survived both rebellions against King Henry I, only to be abandoned soon after the Second Barons' War.

The English Civil Wars of the seventeenth century had little impact on Suffolk's physical landscape, with no major campaigns fought in the county itself. However, the people of Suffolk played an important role on the outcome of many battles, including raising troops and financing the Parliamentary cause. That isn't to say that Suffolk wasn't exposed to disturbances that had the potential to become much more severe. In April 1643, Lowestoft became occupied by Royalist gentry from Suffolk and Norfolk. While Great Yarmouth was securely in the hands of Parliamentary supporters, the Royalists

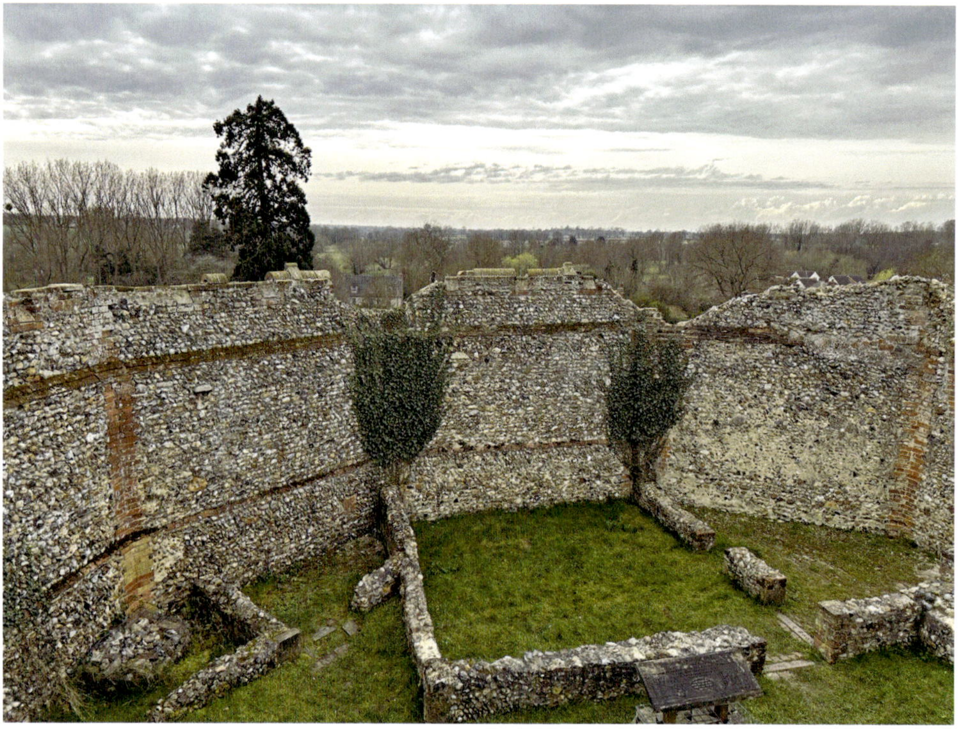

Largely destroyed in 1265, the remains of Eye Castle are one of the few remaining examples of an early Norman motte-and-bailey castle.

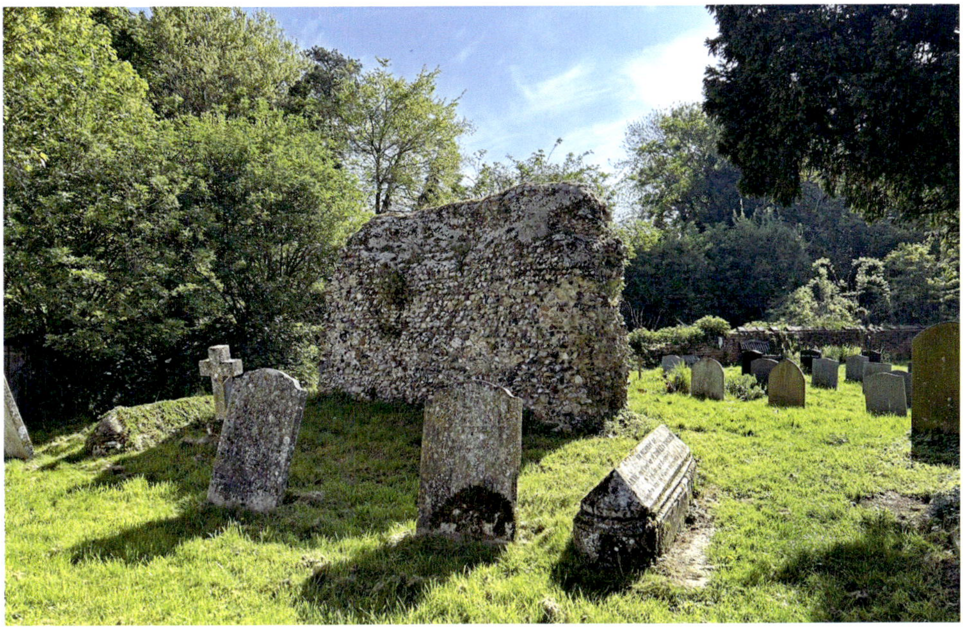

The remains of Lidgate Castle in the churchyard of St Mary's.

believed they could use the port at Lowestoft to acquire foreign arms to use against the Eastern Association's armies. This occupation would be a short-lived affair: when Cromwell left Cambridge with 1,000 troops, they were able to retake Lowestoft almost immediately without a fight. Similarly, in 1648 at Bury St Edmunds, the puritan ban on Maypole dancing led to protests on 12 May. The erection of a Maypole led Lord Fairfax's cavalry to ride into town to disperse the crowd, only for the soldiers to be chased out of the town as people shouted their support for King Charles. The situation escalated when the crowd, now believed to number over 600, decided to seize control of the town's powder magazine. However, within two days the Parliamentary forces had regained control.

For the most part, the Suffolk gentry supported Parliament, either because of the unpopular taxes levied by Charles I or their puritan principles mirrored those of the Parliamentary leader, Oliver Cromwell. In February 1643, the Suffolk Committee – whose role was to raise troops and money for Parliament – formed from the Puritan Suffolk gentry and joined the Eastern Association. Through their business and land ownership they held much of the wealth of the county. The alliance of Suffolk, Norfolk, Essex, Cambridgeshire and Hertfordshire – plus later Lincolnshire and Huntingdonshire – provided an army which fought at the Parliamentary victory of the Battle of Marston Moor in 1644 and a decisive victory at Naseby in June 1645. Across the border in Essex, the men of the Suffolk Trained Bands – Suffolk's militia force – took part in the Siege of Colchester. The Suffolk Trained Bands provided four Regiments of Foot and seven Troops of Horse. Sir Thomas Barnardiston, whose father Sir Nathaniel Barnardiston of Kedington was a wealthy and influential member of the Suffolk Committee, commanded a Regiment for Parliament.

Foreign Foes

While military activity in Suffolk during the early twelfth to the mid-seventeenth centuries was predominantly defined by internal conflicts, from the second half of the seventeenth century, attacks from foreign foes would have a lasting effect on Suffolk's military landscape. The Dutch and French would become familiar adversaries over the next two centuries, and with Britain being an island nation these attacks would come by sea. During this period Suffolk's vast coastline would be the scene of decisive naval battles and amphibious landings, leading to the construction of defensive fortifications that survive to the present day.

Historically, Suffolk had been very lightly defended by permanent and maintained fortifications and while many Tudor defences were proposed, most were never built. Those that were built during this time – at Minsmere, Dunwich, Kessingland, Pakefield and Framlingham – were soon abandoned once the threat of the Spanish Armada

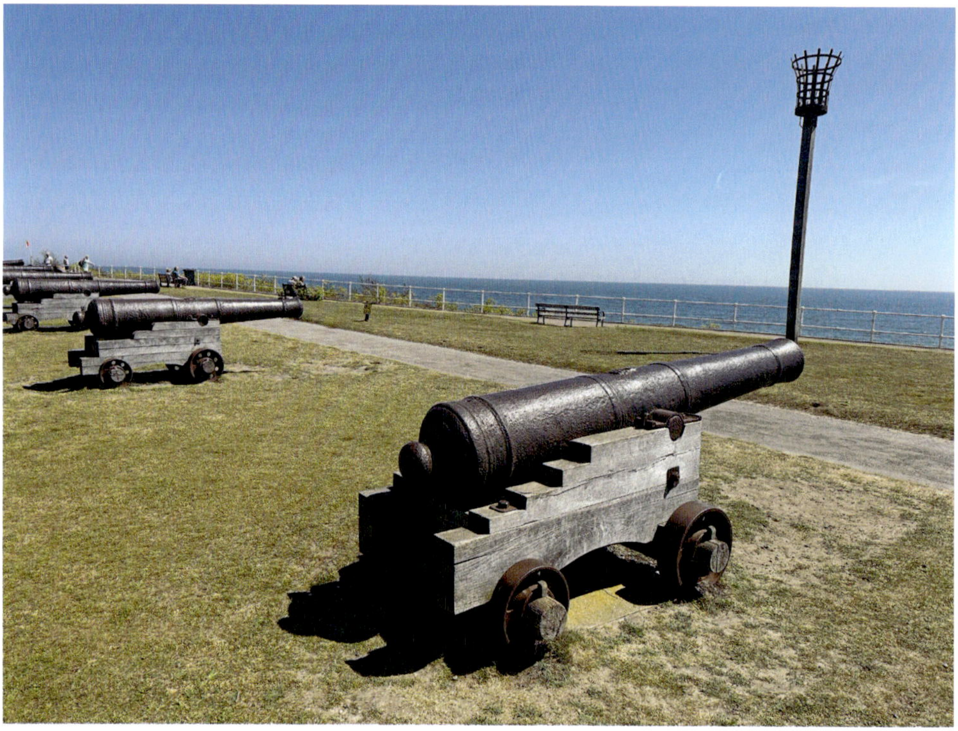

Cannons bearing the Tudor rose on Gun Hill, in a commanding position overlooking the bay at Southwold.

had passed. Dunwich had the county's first defensive work specifically designed for artillery: a bulwark, built at the mouth of Dunwich Haven in 1479. Dunwich had been granted additional artillery in 1569, however when the threat of the Spanish Armada led to Suffolk's coastal defences being reviewed in 1586, the guns were unusable as they had been neither been maintained nor even mounted. While other bulwarks and gun emplacements were erected during the Tudor period, none have survived. It wouldn't be until the seventeenth century that Suffolk's coast was seriously under threat from foreign foes.

There had been years of tension between English and Dutch trade interests during the first half of the seventeenth century, and when Cromwell's Navigation Act of 1651 restricted English trade to English ships, the Dutch saw their position as leader of European trade threatened. The commercial rivalry between the two nations led to the First Anglo-Dutch War between 1552 and 1654, and three more wars from 1665 to 1667, 1672 to 1674, and lastly 1780 to 1784. These wars were predominantly fought at sea, which was fortunate as Suffolk's sprawling beaches and low cliffs made landing an army to march on London an attractive prospect for potential invaders; to make matters worse, very few defence structures had been built to defend the coast. Many of the proposed Tudor defences had never been built, and those that were built were soon abandoned after the threat of the Spanish Armada had passed. It wasn't just the beaches that made Suffolk's coast appealing to would-be invaders; there were also protective bays where they could land their armies. It is probably for this reason that some of the key battles fought against the Dutch occurred off Suffolk's coast. On 2 June 1653, during the First Anglo-Dutch War, the Battle of Gabbard – named after the shoal near Southwold – took place between two evenly matched navies: the English had 100 ships and five fireships; the Dutch had ninety-eight ships and six fireships. The two-day battle resulted in a decisive English victory and would ultimately lead to the English blockade of the Dutch coast. The Battle of Gabbard was of particular significance in the history of British naval warfare, for it was the first time an English navy fought in a single line formation, concentrating firepower on a decisive part of the enemy's fleet.

During the Second Anglo-Dutch War, the Suffolk coast was once again the scene of a great naval battle. On 13 June 1665, the first naval action of the war resulted in the clash of over 200 ships from the English and Dutch navies at the Battle of Lowestoft. This battle, as the name suggests, took place off the coast of Lowestoft (albeit some 30 miles off the coast) and occurred when Admiral Jacob van Wassenaer Obdam led a Dutch fleet into English waters to prevent the English navy from blockading their ports once again. Amongst the English fleet, the *Royal Charles* – which had on board James, Duke of York (later King James II) – engaged with the Dutch flagship *Eendracht* before the Dutch vessel exploded, killing Admiral Wassenaer. Some thirty-plus Dutch ships were destroyed or captured; however, the success of the *Royal Charles* would be short-lived. In June 1667, a Dutch fleet entered the Thames estuary and raided along the River Medway until it reached Chatham and Gillingham. Here, several English ships of the line were anchored, including the *Royal Charles*. The role this ship played during the Battle of Lowestoft was not lost on the Dutch fleet, so the *Royal Charles* was captured and towed back to The Netherlands. This war trophy became a public attraction until it was scrapped a few years later. The same Dutch fleet that raided the Medway would soon look for targets along the east coast, particularly the Royal dockyard at Harwich.

To take Harwich, the Dutch navy needed to ensure that the fort at Landguard – Harwich's outermost defence – posed no risk to its fleet. The Dutch fleet, under the command of Admiral de Ruyter, tried to bombard Landguard in early July 1667, however the dangerous waters near the fort made it impossible to fire upon the fort with any accuracy. Two attempts were made by Dutch troops to take Landguard on 2 July 1667, however its garrison of 200 men under the command of Captain Nathaniel Darrell were able to repel the attackers, which ultimately forced the Dutch to abandon their plans to assault Harwich. The attack on Landguard proved to be the last opposed amphibious invasion of England. The fort that survives today was constructed after this famous attack, and contains elements built between 1717 and 1720. The enlarged pentagonal-shaped fort was built in 1750 in response to threats from the French and the Jacobean rebellion in Scotland; alterations were made between 1870 and the 1890s with an upgrade of the armaments to rifled muzzle-loading guns and 10-inch and 6-inch hydro-pneumatic breach-loading guns; final changes were made in the early 1900s with the addition of 6-inch and 4.7-inch with quick-fire guns.

It was during the Third Anglo-Dutch War that Suffolk witnessed one the closest naval battles to its shores. A Dutch fleet – once again under the command of Admiral de

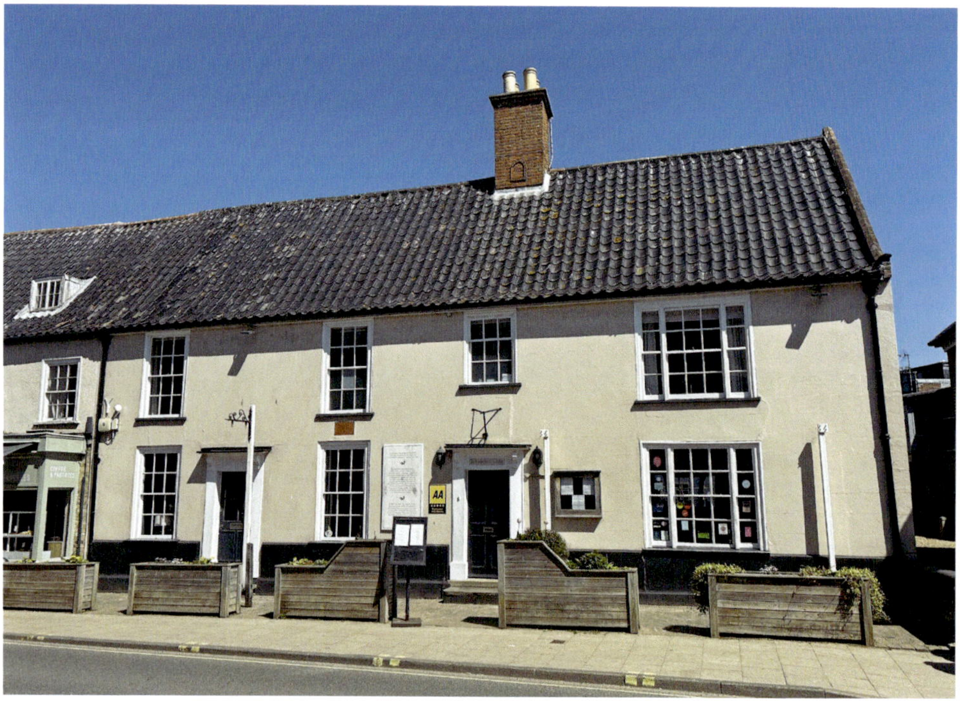

Sutherland House in Southwold. The headquarters for the Duke of York and Earl of Sandwich prior to the Battle of Solebay, and now a bed and breakfast where guests can stay in the room once used by the man who would become King of England.

Ruyter – advanced on a fleet of English and French ships that lay at anchor in Solebay, now known as Southwold, on 28 May 1672. The fleet received news of an impending assault the evening before but ignored the recommendations made by Admiral Edward Montagu, Earl of Sandwich; the English fleet's commander, the Duke of York, failed to take the English fleet to sea to avoid being caught at anchor. The Battle of Solebay began in the early hours of 28 May. The ferocious battle led crowds from the coastal town to gather on the cliffs to watch the billows of clouds coming from ships set ablaze. The most significant English loss was that of the *Royal James*, the Earl of Sandwich's flagship. After the battle, hundreds of injured and dead sailors – including the body of the Earl of Sandwich – were washed ashore along the Suffolk coast. Sutherland House, one of the few properties to survive Lowestoft's fire of 1659, was used by the Duke of York and the Earl of Sandwich while their fleet remained at anchor.

Landguard is not the only surviving fortification built along the Suffolk coast. Between 1805 and 1812, 103 Martello towers were built to defend the south-east coast from a possible Napoleonic invasion. Eighteen were built to protect the Suffolk coastline,

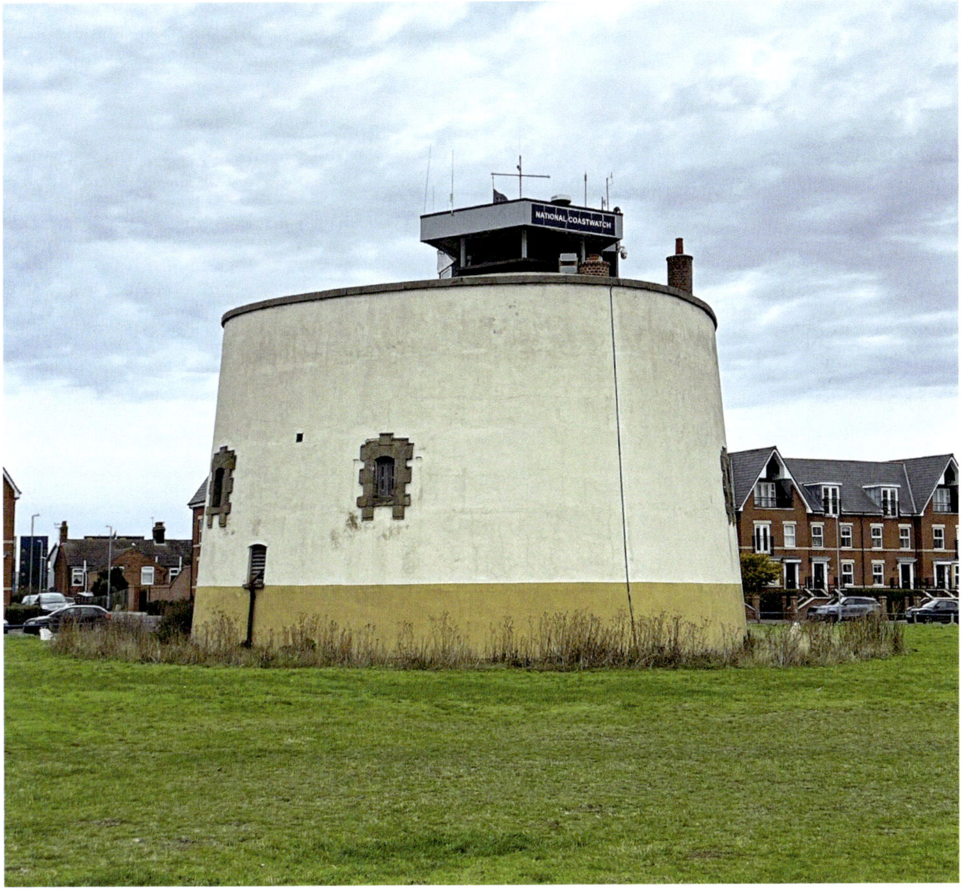

Martello tower 'P 'at Felixstowe, now a lookout station for the National Coastwatch Institution.

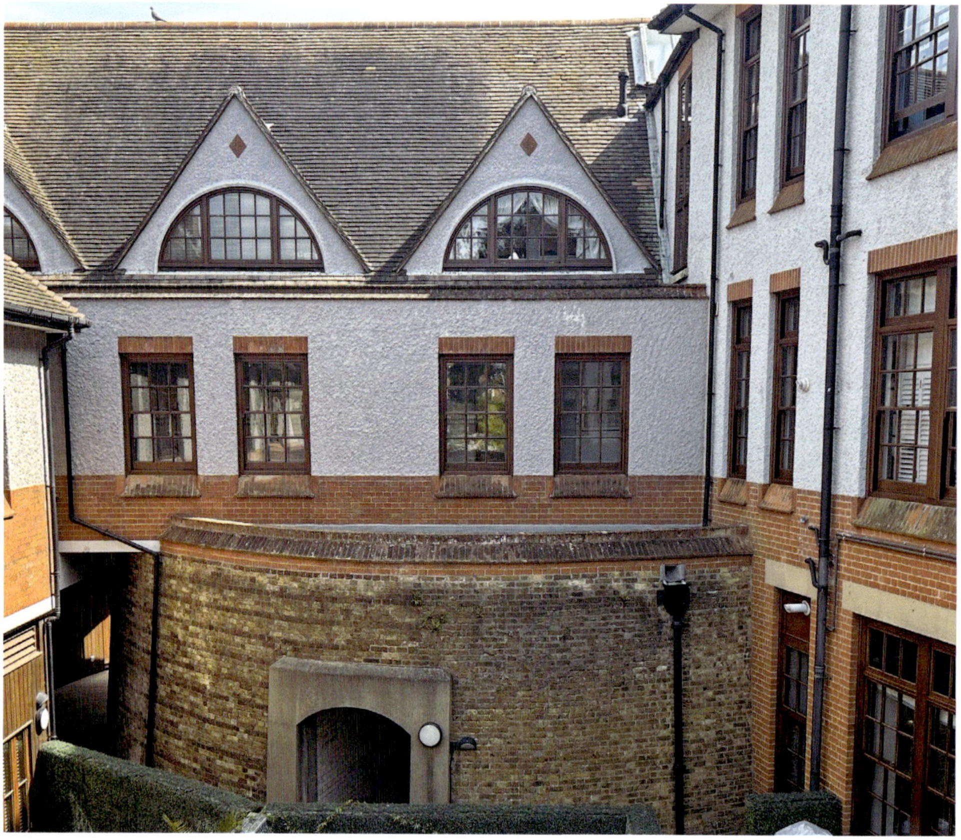

Martello tower at the former Bartlett Hospital, Felixstowe. The hospital closed in 2006, and the building was redeveloped into flats in 2013.

from Shotley Point to Aldeburgh. Only forty-five of those original Martello towers survive today, with almost a quarter of them located along the Suffolk coast. Based on the design of the fifteenth-century Corsican fort that defied attempts by the Royal Navy to reduce it to rubble, the towers in Suffolk were built in the standard east coast style. They comprised of three levels: a platform on the roof that had a 24-pounder, smooth bore, muzzle-loading gun mounted and two 24-pounder cannonades or two 5.5-inch howitzers to repel invaders; the first floor provided accommodation for those garrisoned; and provisions and munitions were stored in the basement. The tower would house a garrison of twenty-four men and an officer in charge, who had the relative luxury of his own room with a window and fireplace. Thanks to Admiral Nelson's decisive victory over the French navy at the Battle of Trafalgar, no sooner had construction been completed on the Martello towers then the immediate threat of invasion had passed. Eleven of the eighteen towers built along the Suffolk coast remain fully intact today. Towers 'L' and 'M' on Shotley Point stand on the former HMS Ganges site, however both are surmounted by water tanks. Tower 'P', to the south of Felixstowe town, was handed over to the coastguard in 1816, and is now used as a lookout station for the National Coastwatch Institution.

During the First World War, Tower 'P' was used a Naval Wireless Station for the Royal Navy's Harwich Force of light cruisers and destroyers. Towers 'N', 'O', 'S', 'V', 'X' and 'BB' were either demolished or lost to the sea. Interestingly, Tower 'R' partially survives: it was built into Bartlett Hospital, above Undercliff Road East in Felixstowe, although this portion of the tower is now only half its original height. Thankfully, five of Suffolk's surviving Martello towers have been restored and adapted for modern living. Towers 'Q', 'U', 'W', 'Y' and 'AA' have been converted into private homes. Located at Slaughden, near Aldeburgh, Tower 'CC' is a unique quatrefoil design of four interlocking, clover-shaped towers surrounded by a dry moat.

While Suffolk's early eighteenth-century military heritage was dominated by the construction of fortifications along its coast to defend from invasion, Suffolk-born soldiers and sailors were engaged in military service across the globe. Many of these accounts will be discussed in the next chapter, however it is worth noting that during the Napoleonic invasion threat, Britain was momentarily at war with one of France's allies, with which Britain had a complicated recent history – the United States of America. During the War of 1812, the Royal Navy and British Army were engaged in battles on the other side of the Atlantic. Captain Philip Broke of Broke Hall, Nacton, was in command of the Royal Navy frigate *Shannon* in August 1806. Broke was ordered to Halifax, Canada, and was tasked with intercepting American shipping along the western Atlantic in 1812. During

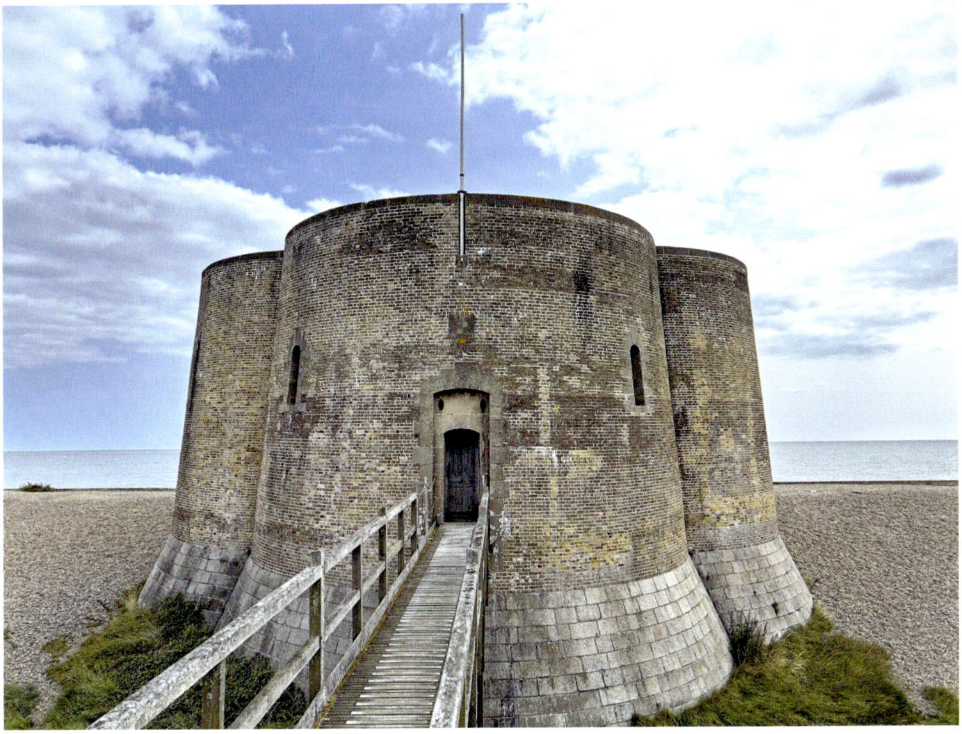

The unique quatrefoil-shaped Martello tower near Aldeburgh, now owned by The Landmark Trust, which allows the tower to be used as a holiday home.

this period Royal Navy gunnery was often poor, so Broke spent his time commanding the *Shannon*, improving the ship's standards of gunnery. In late May of 1813, Broke was sent to keep watch on Boston Harbour, where on 1 June he engaged the American frigate *USS Chesapeake*. The *Chesapeake* – one of six frigates authorised by Congress with passage of the Naval Act of 1794 – was captained by James Lawrence, who had only taken command of the ship twelve days prior. His crew was inexperienced with many members who had never participated in naval battles. As crowds amassed near the harbour, they watched the *Chesapeake* succumb to the attacks by the experienced and well-trained crew of the *Shannon*, and the ship was captured in fifteen minutes. Broke, having been severely wounded during the attack, returned to England with the *Shannon* in October 1813. The wound he received during the battle would continue to trouble him and he would never serve at sea again, spending the rest of his life at Broke Hall before being buried in St Marin's Church in Nacton.

Renewed fears of invasion from France led to efforts to re-fortify the Suffolk coast in the early 1860s. Shotley Battery was built between 1862 and 1865 to supplement the existing Martello towers at Shotley Point. In 1873, the battery gun emplacements were adapted to house 7-inch rifled muzzled-loading guns, and the battery would see further alterations to its firepower, with new emplacements, enlarged protective earthworks, and subterranean shell magazines. Shotley Battery and the surrounding site was transferred

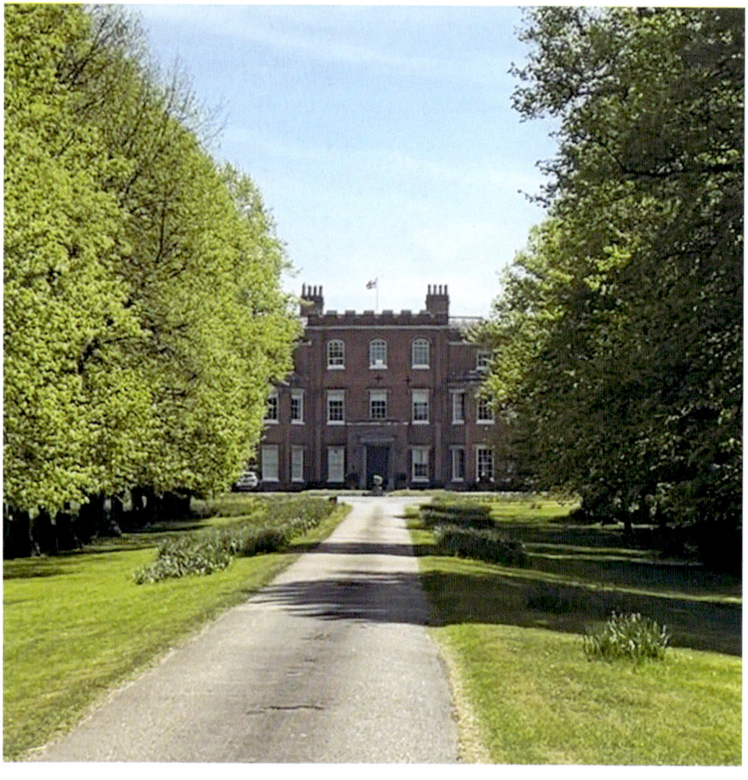

Broke Hall, the home of Philip Broke who captured the USS *Chesapeake* during the War of 1812. In recognition of his victory, Broke was made a baronet in September 1813, knighted in January 1815, and promoted to rear-admiral in July 1830.

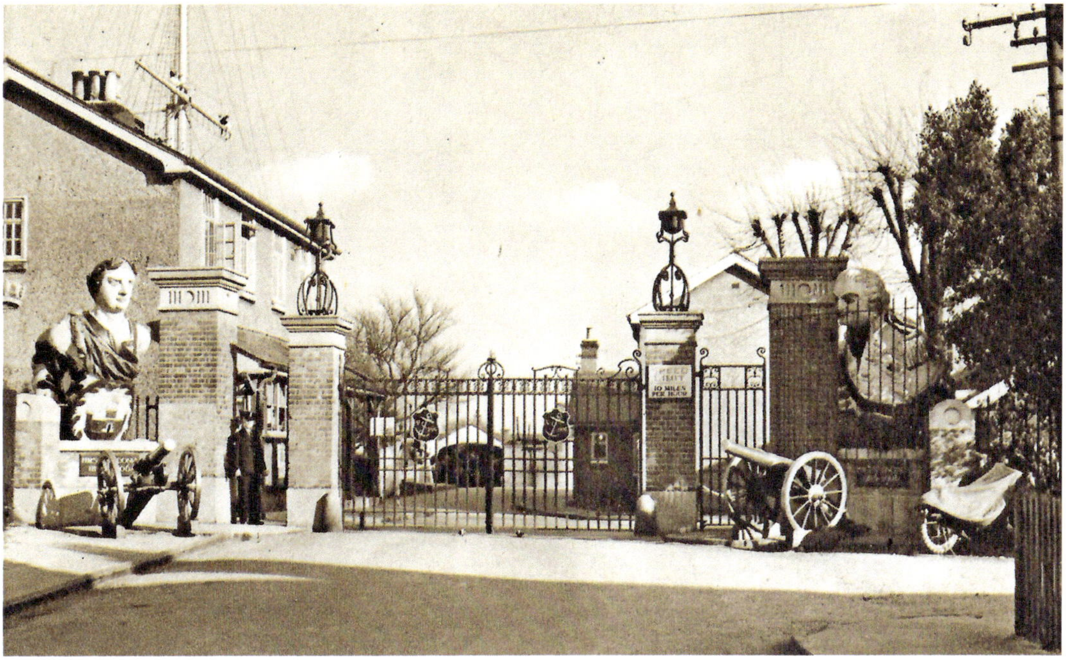

The main entrance to HMS Ganges at Shotley Gate, *c.* 1900.

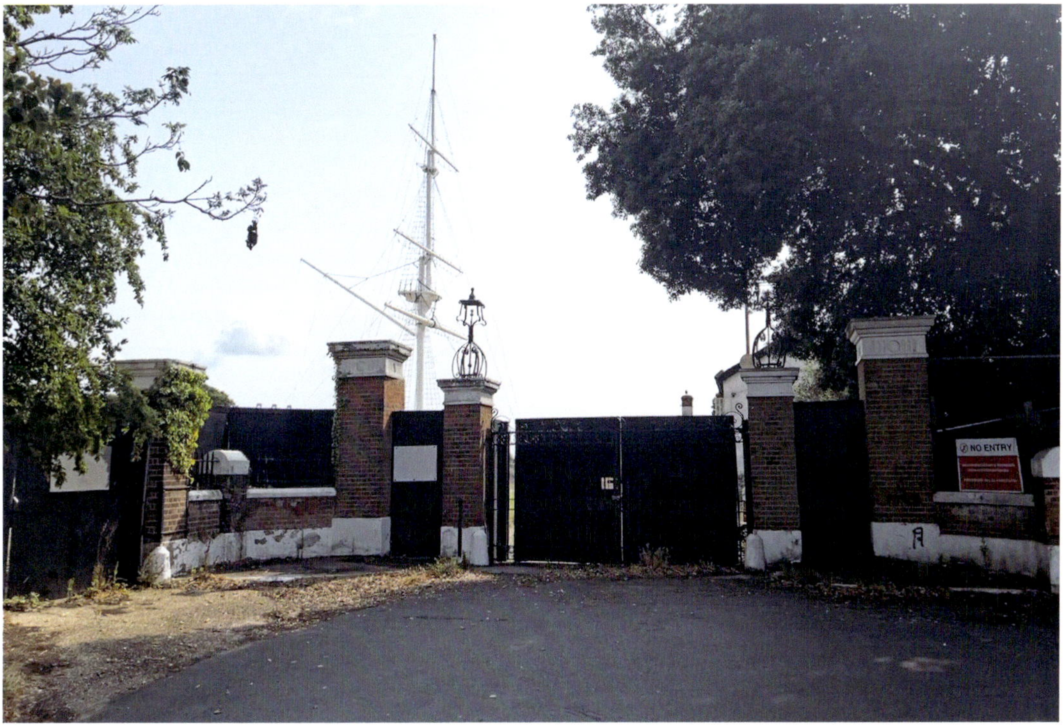

Shotley Gate main entrance at present day.

to the Royal Naval Training Establishment (RNTE) in 1904 and renamed HMS Ganges in 1927. The RNTE closed in 1976, and the site was used for police training.

In the late nineteenth century, it wasn't just fortifications that were built in Suffolk to defend the coast. In the 1870s, it was decided that the harbour at Harwich in neighbouring Essex was a suitable location to deploy mines. The Submarine Mining Establishment (SME) was established in 1871. This was a specialist branch of the Royal Engineers that was responsible for the training of hundreds of men in deploying and maintaining these underwater mine fields. Between 1877 and 1880, an SME facility was built adjacent to the northern outworks of Landguard Fort. The SME main building – the Ravelin Block – stored and transported mines along a narrow-gauge railway to a nearby jetty, from where they were deployed. Once the mines were in position, they could be detonated by using electric cables from a testing room in Landguard Fort. Although the Admiralty took over mining operations in 1905, the Ravelin Block continued to be used by the Royal Engineers for their other responsibilities in the area, such as maintaining searchlight and communications systems.

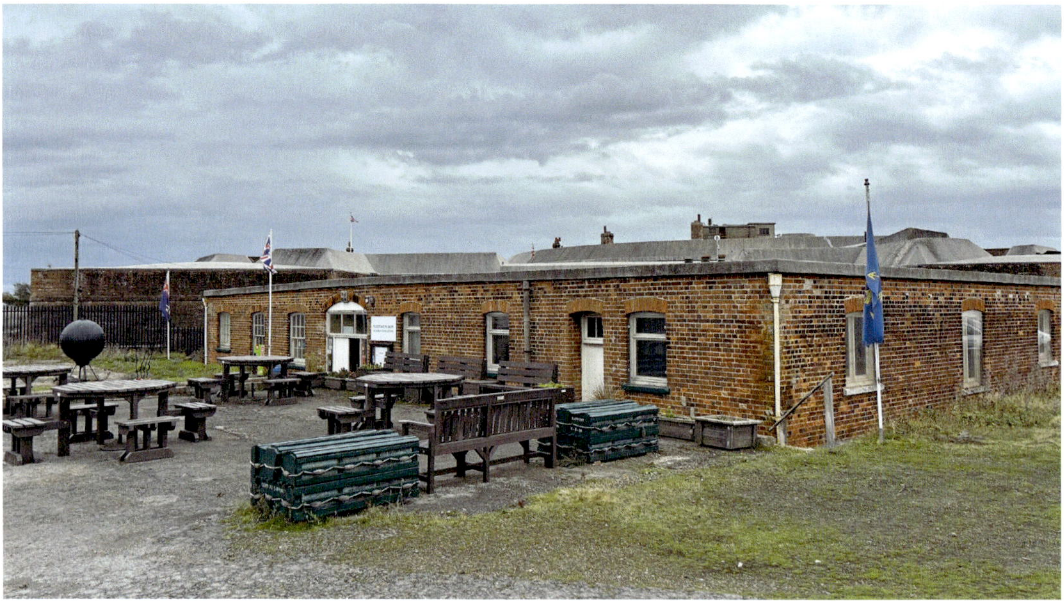

The Ravelin Building near Landguard Fort, the former home to the Submarine Mining Establishment. This now houses the Felixstowe Museum, where many of the building's mining operation features are on display, including a section of the original narrow-gauge railway track that ran throughout the building.

Regulars and Militia

Over the centuries, Suffolk has been home to many military units. Some have stayed briefly in temporary camps established when invasion posed a real threat; others stayed while their ships were repaired, and sailors could take advantage of what was offered in the local towns. The county welcomed thousands of servicemen and women who served during the First and Second World Wars. Some were attached to unit headquarters and training facilities, others were patients at hospitals and convalescent homes, and many more were simply waiting to be deployed overseas. However, of all the regular military units associated with Suffolk, none is more famous than the Suffolk Regiment, affectionately known as 'The Old Dozen'. The Childers reforms of 1881 reorganised the infantry regiments in the British Army by merging two regular army battalions into one regiment which would then be affiliated with an entire county. The 12th Regiment of Foot, which already had two battalions and was not required to merge with any additional units, was renamed the Suffolk Regiment. However, this was not the earliest connection between the county of Suffolk and the 12th Foot. The 12th Regiment of Foot was first formed in 1685 when Henry Howard, 7th Duke of Norfolk, was ordered by King James II to supress a rebellion led by the Duke of Monmouth. Those recruited for this newly raised force were predominantly from Norfolk and Suffolk, however within their ranks was a company of experienced men who had seen military service in the American colony of Virginia. In its early years, the regiment would see active service in Ireland, including the Battle of the Boyne in 1690. The Regiment was at the fortress at Dixmude, in Belgium, when it became besieged by the French in 1695. The English forces soon surrendered and the entire Regiment, then known as 'Colonel Brewer's Regiment', was captured. They were, however, soon released under a prisoner exchange scheme. The eighteenth century would fare much better for the Regiment, as two of its earliest – and arguably most iconic – battle honours were earned: 'Dettingen' and 'Minden'. In 1743, during the War of the Austrian Succession, the regiment was placed at the centre of the British leading line at the Battle of Dettingen. In front of them, King George II led them into battle where they routed the French, a rare distinction for the Regiment as this would be the last time an English monarch would lead English forces into battle. The Battle of Minden was fought in 1759, as part of the Seven Years' War (1756–63), where British troops fought alongside their Prussian allies under Prince Ferdinand of Brunswick. On the day of the battle, the British and Prussian armies – although outnumbered – defeated the French army on the plains to the northwest of Minden, Germany. It is said that when travelling through German villages on their way to the battle, the regiment picked roses and placed them in their headdresses.

From its creation in 1685 until the army reforms of 1751, the regiment that was initially known as 'Henry, Duke of Norfolk's Regiment' would be known by the names of the various other colonels who commanded the regiment. From 1751 onwards, infantry regiments would be known by a number (allocated by seniority), or date in which they were raised, and not by the name of their colonel. Recognising it as one of the oldest regiments in the British Army, the regiment became known as the 12th Regiment of Foot. In 1769, the Regiment began its fourteen years of service on Gibraltar, where as part of its garrison it successfully defended the country during the great siege of 1779–83. In recognition of its service during the defence of Gibraltar, the Regiment was granted the battle honour 'Gibraltar' and adopted the Castle and Key crest along with the motto 'Montis Insignia Calpe'. In 1782, the Regiment's name would begin to be associated with the county, becoming the 12th (East Suffolk) Regiment of Foot. However, the regiment did not spend much time in Suffolk, nor for that matter England. Having set sail for India in 1796, they spent time in the Caribbean, Flanders and the Netherlands. In 1799, the Regiment fought in the campaign against Tippoo Sultan, the ruler of the state of Mysore (in modern-day India); storming his stronghold at 'Seringapatam' earned them a battle honour by that name. In 1812 – in response to the Napoleonic Wars – a second battalion was raised; however they were disbanded after six years having spent most of their existence in Ireland. After the Napoleonic Wars the Regiment spent time in Ireland before being once again stationed in Gibraltar and Mauritius. In 1848, a second 'reserve' battalion was formed and sent to South Africa for the Eighth Kaffir War (1850–53), earning the battle honour of 'South Africa 1851-52-53'. It was also during this war that the ill-fated troop transport *Birkenhead*, which was carrying fifty-seven reinforcements for the regiment, sank en route in 1852. This will be discussed in greater detail in a later chapter. When the 'Reserve' Battalion returned to England in 1858, it was increased in size and formally became the Regiment's 2nd Battalion. The 1st Battalion would next be on active service overseas in 1854, when it was sent to Australia to help supress the Eureka Rebellion in Victoria, before travelling to New Zealand where it served during the New Zealand Wars in 1860. After returning to India in 1867, the 1st Battalion served during the Second Afghan War. For its service in New Zealand and Afghanistan the Regiment received its last two battle honours under the name the 12th Regiment of Foot.

In 1881, the Childers Reforms led the 12th Regiment of Foot to be affiliated with the entire county of Suffolk. It was subsequently renamed the Suffolk Regiment, and was assigned a Regimental Depot in Bury St Edmunds. The reforms required single battalion regiments to merge, but as the 12th already had two battalions they were not affected. The newly renamed Suffolk Regiment saw its first active service during the Second Boer War (1899–1902), where in January 1900 the 1st Battalion conducted a night attack on the heights near Colesberg. When the four companies – some 354 men – climbed the hill in the dark they came under intense small arms fire, resulting in the loss of their commanding officer and almost half of their men being killed, wounded or taken prisoner. The Regiment was also granted their first post-Childers Reforms battle honour: 'South Africa, 1899–1902'.

At the outbreak of the First World War in 1914, the 1st Battalion was serving in Sudan and would arrive in France in early 1915 before being redirected to Salonika, where they remained for the entire campaign. The 2nd Battalion formed part of the British Expeditionary Force (BEF) which was sent to France in August 1914, serving on the

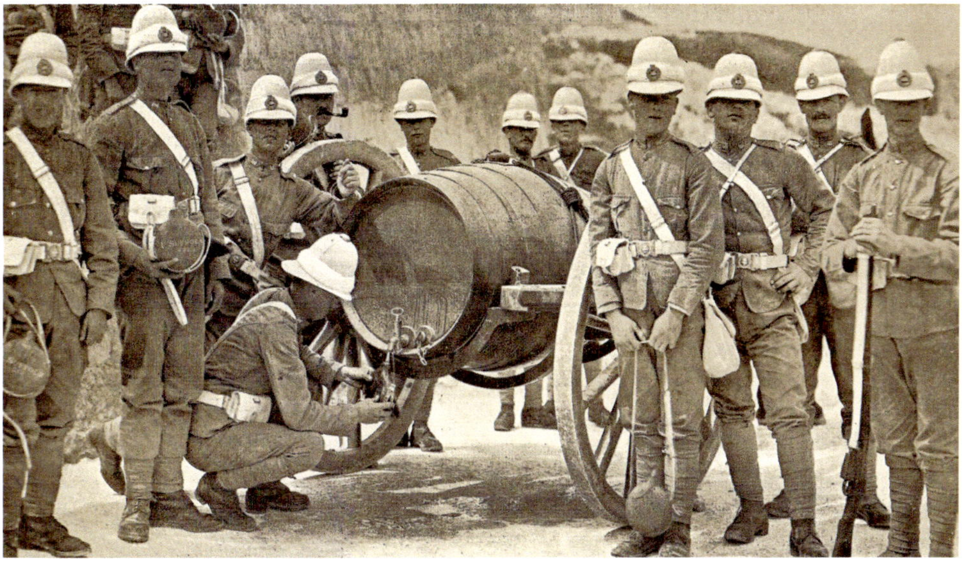

Soldiers of the 1st Battalion Suffolk Regiment in the field during the Boer War, showing how the water was resupplied to those on outpost duty.

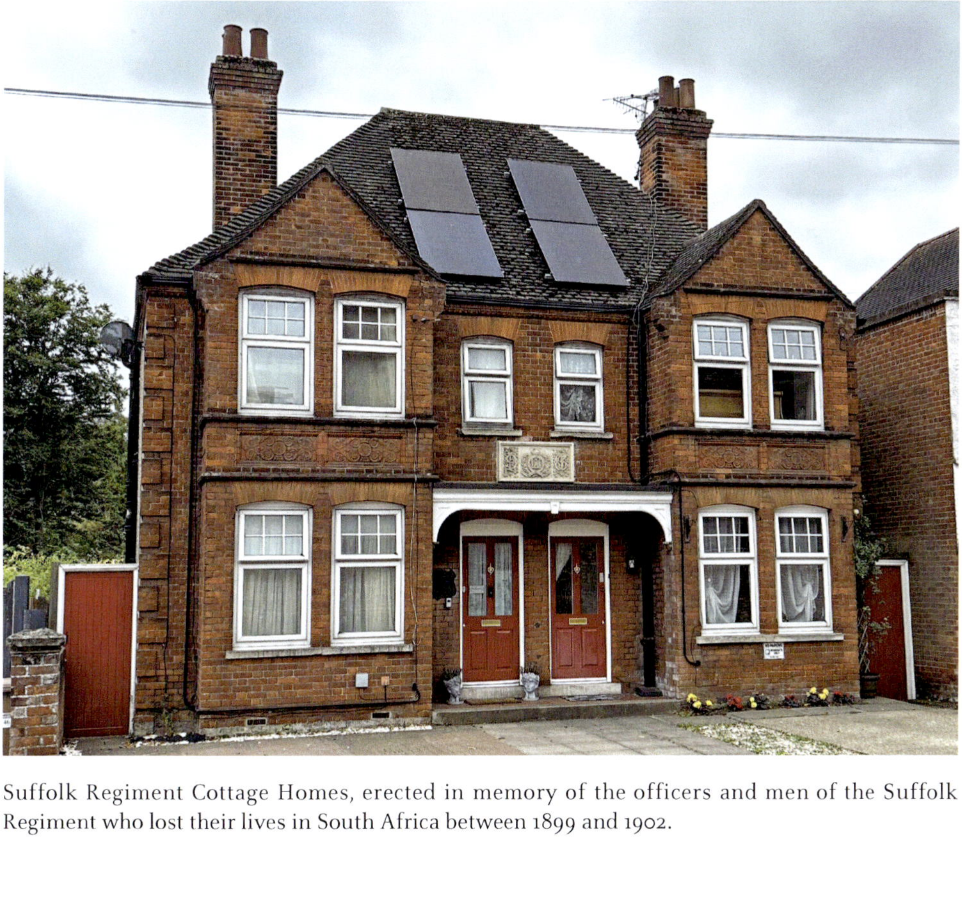

Suffolk Regiment Cottage Homes, erected in memory of the officers and men of the Suffolk Regiment who lost their lives in South Africa between 1899 and 1902.

Western Front for the duration of the war. The Suffolk Regiment expanded to twenty-three battalions during the war; the 7th to 12th Battalions formed part of Kitchener's New Army, and all served on the Western Front. The Suffolk Regiment were present in all theatres and at major battles throughout the war, with two of its soldiers earning the Victoria Cross. These were Sergeant Arthur Frederick Saunders and Corporal Sidney James Day, the former of who's medal is proudly displayed at the Suffolk Regiment Museum in Bury St Edmunds.

During the interwar years, the 1st Battalion served in India and Malta and ultimately arrived back in England before the outbreak of the Second World War. It went straight to France as part of the BEF, however found itself being evacuated from Dunkirk in May the following year. The Battalion returned to France on D-Day in 1944 and fought across North-West Europe to Germany until the end of the war. The 2nd Battalion was in Ireland in the early 1920s and, after a few years in England, was stationed in Gibraltar, then China and finally India in 1939, where they remained protecting the North-West Frontier at the outbreak of war. It continued to serve on home defence duties in India, along the North-West Frontier, until it joined the Burma Campaign and fought at Arakan and Imphal in 1944.

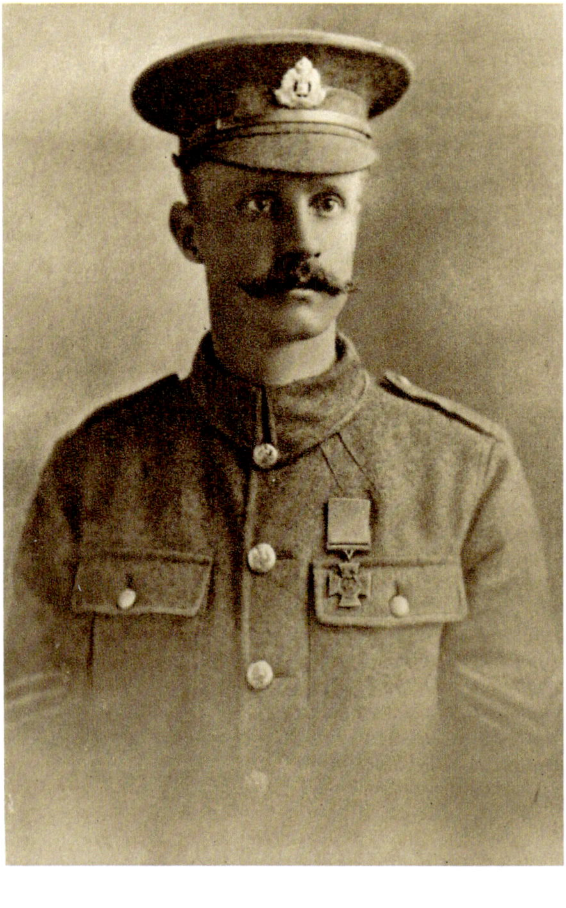

Sergeant Arthur Frederick Saunders VC, 9th Battalion Suffolk Regiment. On 26 September 1915, near Loos, Saunders held back advancing German troops – despite being severely wounded – using a machine gun, while his own Battalion were forced to retire.

After the Second World War, the 1st Battalion served overseas in Egypt, Palestine, Greece and then Malaya, while the 2nd Battalion was disbanded in 1948. The 1st Battalion returned home for a short time in 1953, before moving to Germany and then on to the Battalion's final overseas deployment in Cyprus in 1956. The Battalion returned home in 1959, and on the 29 August 1959 was amalgamated with the 1st Battalion of the Norfolk Regiment to form the 1st East Anglian Regiment. In 1967, this would in turn be converted into a battalion of The Royal Anglian Regiment. Despite these amalgamations and name changes, The Royal Anglian Regiment continues to recruit in the same areas as its predecessors: Suffolk, Norfolk, Essex and Cambridge. The legacy of The Suffolk Regiment – its honours and traditions – continue to be recognised by their successors. The 'Castle and Key' insignia, for example, which featured on the Suffolk Regiment's cap badge was adopted by the Royal Anglian Regiment (RAR). The Regiment's motto of 'Stabilis' (Steady) was the family motto of a former colonel, Scipio Duroure. The 1st Battalion RAR commemorates the 12th Regiment's participation in the Battle of Minden through its annual Minden Day celebration, where the 'Minden Rose' is worn in regimental headdress.

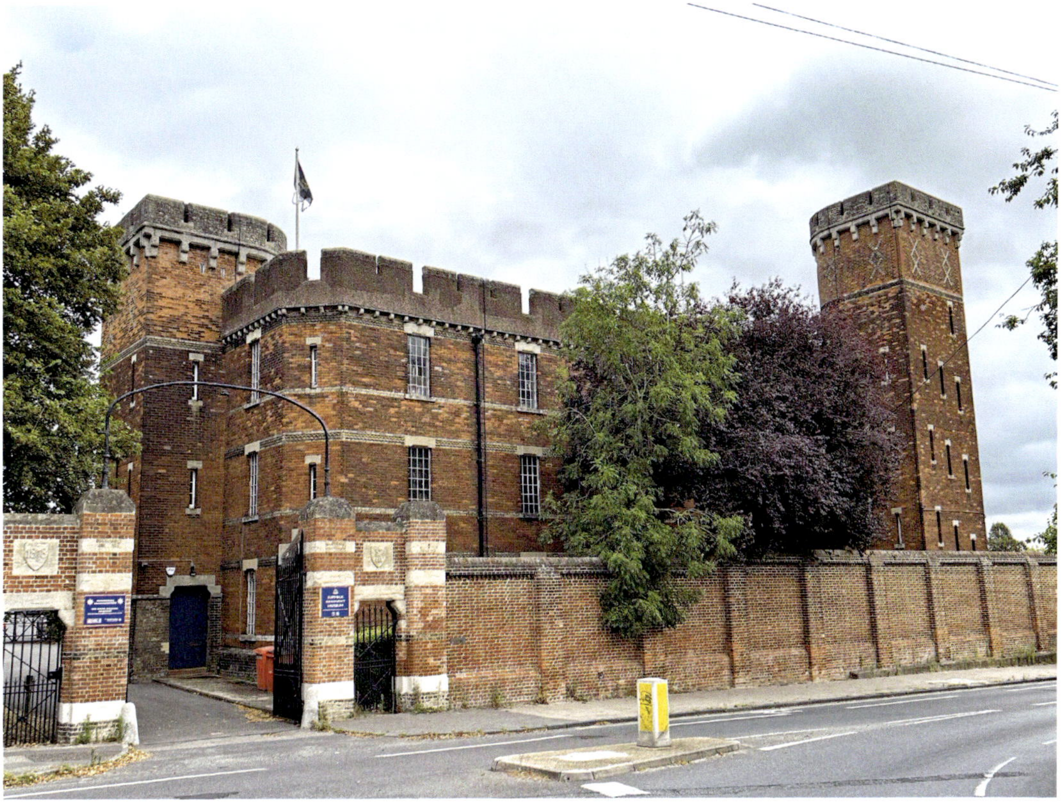

The former armoury of the Suffolk Regiment at the Gibraltar barracks now houses the Suffolk Regiment Museum, while its upper floors are the home of the Regimental Headquarters of the Royal Anglian Regiment.

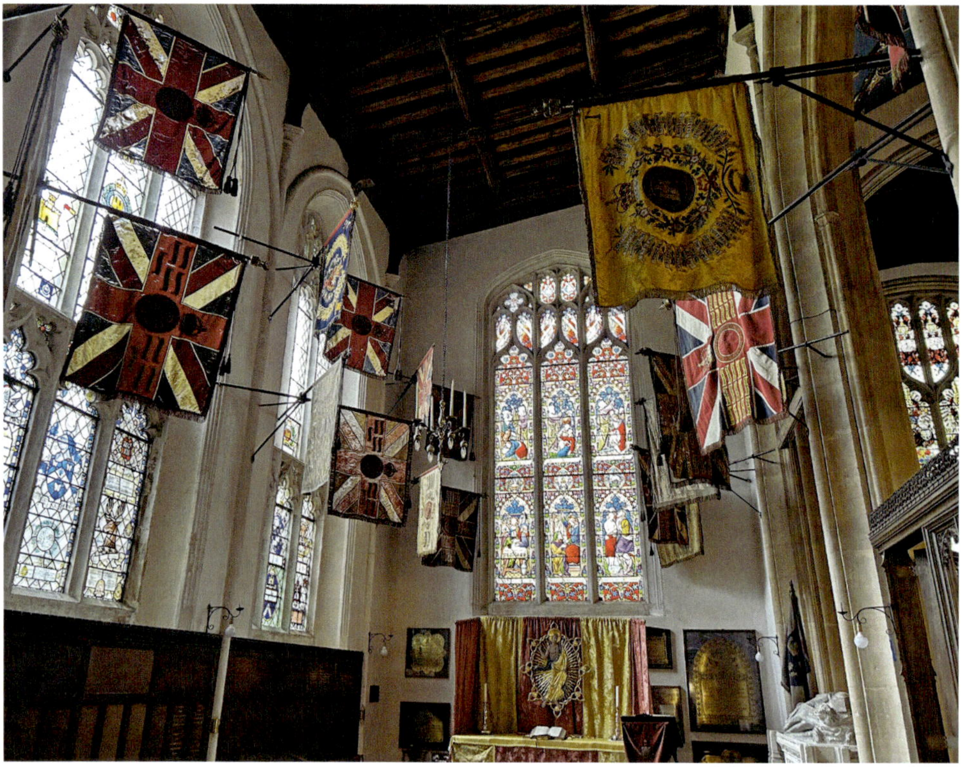

Regimental Colours on display inside the Regimental Chapel at St Mary's Church, Bury St Edmunds.

Militia units in Suffolk predate their Regular Army counterparts. While this chapter explores the Regular and Milita forces that originated in Suffolk, the term 'militia' is used in its broadest definition: part-time soldiers that are generally mobilised for a specific military purpose. For this reason, other units which broadly fall under this definition (such as Trained Bands, Volunteer Rifle Corps and Yeomanry) will be discussed individually, but for the remainder of this chapter will also be considered as 'militia'. Similar to the Regular Army, the names and organisational structure of militia units, as well as their function, changed over time.

The earliest form of militia in Suffolk can be traced back to the Trained Bands that were established in the mid-sixteenth century and were mustered to defend the country's shores when the threat of invasion was deemed likely. The Suffolk Trained Bands (STB) mustered in 1588 when the threat from the Spanish Armada led to the militia being posted to vulnerable positions along Suffolk's coast: over 2,000 men of the STB joined Queen Elizabeth's army at Tilbury. During the Second English Civil War, the STB once again crossed the border into Essex and assisted Cromwell's army during the Siege of Colchester in June 1648. Parliament passed new Militia Acts in 1648 and 1650 which saw the Trained Bands begin to be known more commonly as the militia, and replaced the King's Lord-Lieutenant with Parliament appointed commissioners to control them. However, The Militia Act of 1661 re-established the King's Lord-Lieutenant as having

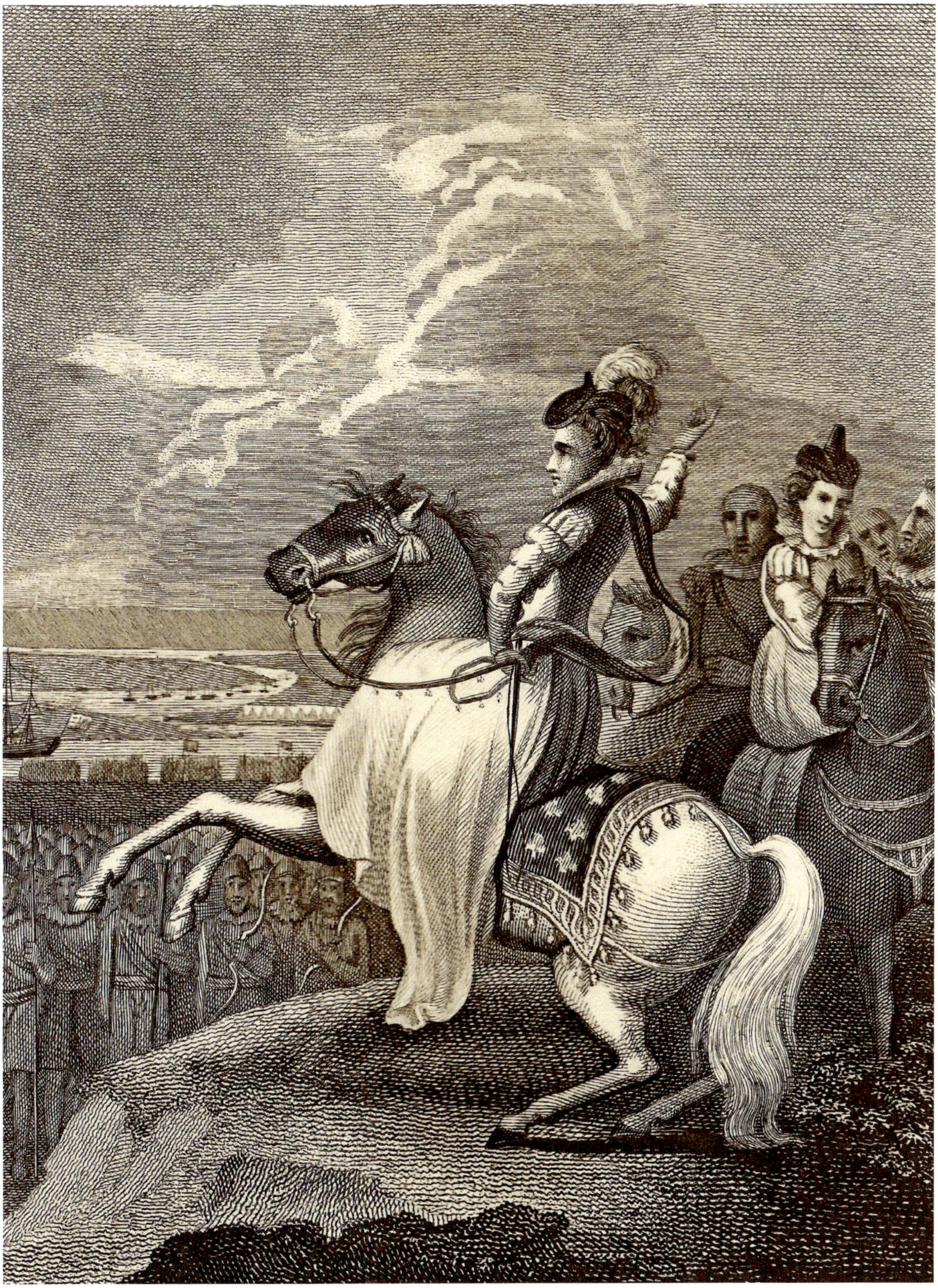

Queen Elizabeth at Tilbury, where some 2,000 members of the Suffolk Trained Bands met to face the threat of invasion.

control of the militia following the Restoration of the Monarchy. In 1667, men from the Suffolk Militia supported Captain Nathaniel Darrell's Lord High Admirals' Regiment at Landguard Fort. When the Dutch forces attacked the fort, the militia attacked the invaders' landing area, forcing their retreat. In 1759, the county's militia would be known by their 'West' and 'East' county prefixes. The West Suffolk Militia's headquarters was at Bury St Edmunds, while the East Suffolk Militia were based at Ipswich. In 1852, additional reforms to the Militia Act saw the creation of artillery militia units, allowing regular Royal Artillery units manning coastal defences to be used for overseas service. In 1853, the East Suffolk Militia retrained to become the Suffolk Artillery Militia, with five batteries based at Ipswich where, in 1855, a new barracks was built for them at what is now Geneva and Cecil Road.

The Cardwell and Childers Reforms of the 1870s and 1881 would have a significant impact on the administration and organisation of Suffolk's Militia and Volunteer Rifle Corps (the latter of which will be discussed later in this chapter). It was hoped that these reforms would help link regular infantry regiments with specific localities, encourage local recruitment and connect the regular army with the militia. The country was divided into sixty-six infantry districts, each with its own regimental depot. Suffolk was the 32nd Brigade Depot between 1873 and 1881 when it then became the 12th Regimental District. In 1878, a new Regimental Depot was built on a 15-acre site in Bury St Edmunds. Gibraltar Barracks, named after the 12th Regiment's first battle honour, would in 1881 become the depot for the newly formed Suffolk Regiment. The Suffolk Regiment included the two regular infantry battalions of the 12th Foot; the West Suffolk Militia became the 3rd (Militia) Battalion of the Suffolk Regiment; and the Cambridgeshire Militia became the regiment's 4th (Militia) Battalion, while Suffolk's volunteer force became Volunteer Battalions of the Suffolk Regiment. In 1907, additional reforms by the Secretary State for War, Richard Haldane, created the Territorial Forces Act which redesignated militia units as Special Reserve.

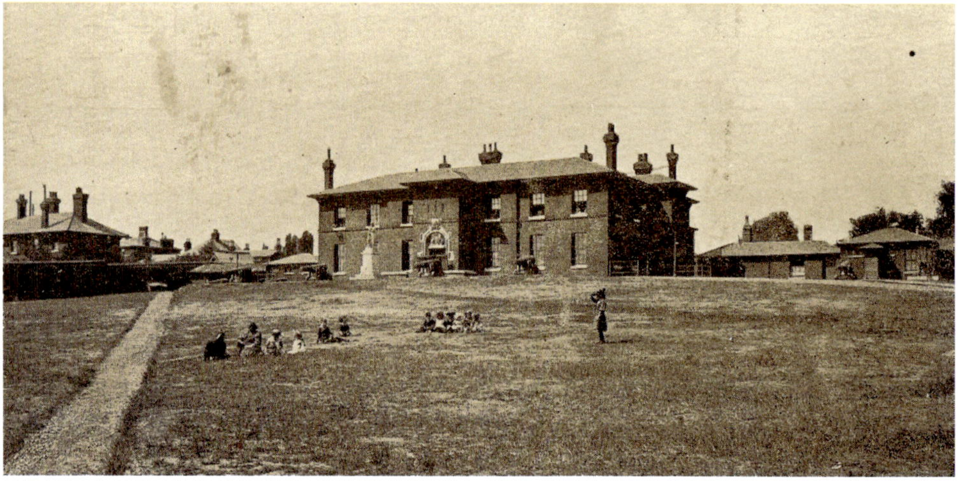

The Militia Depot (now demolished) at Ipswich at the turn of the twentieth century.

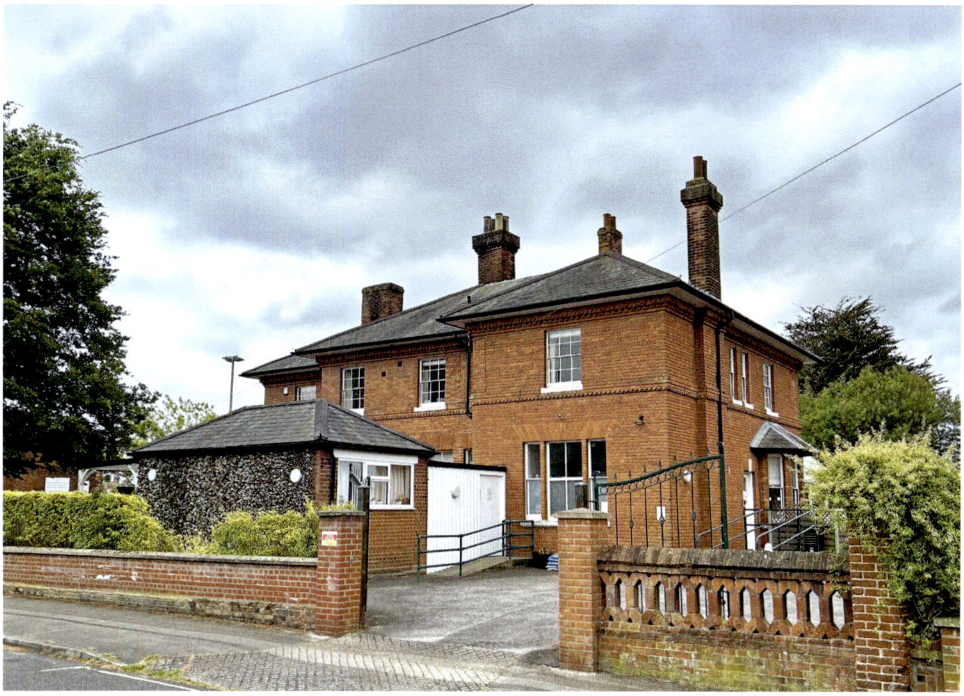

The former Adjutant's house of the Militia Barracks along Ivry Road, Ipswich.

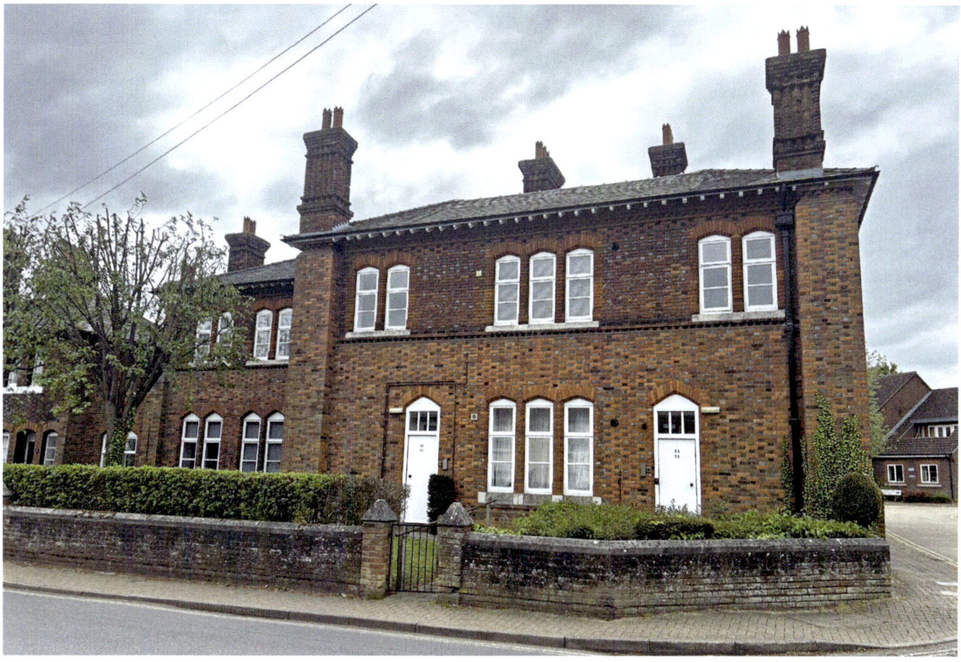

Part of the barracks of the West Suffolk Militia Building built in 1857 on Kings Road, Bury St Edmunds. It became the headquarters of the Suffolk Yeomanry in the early twentieth century.

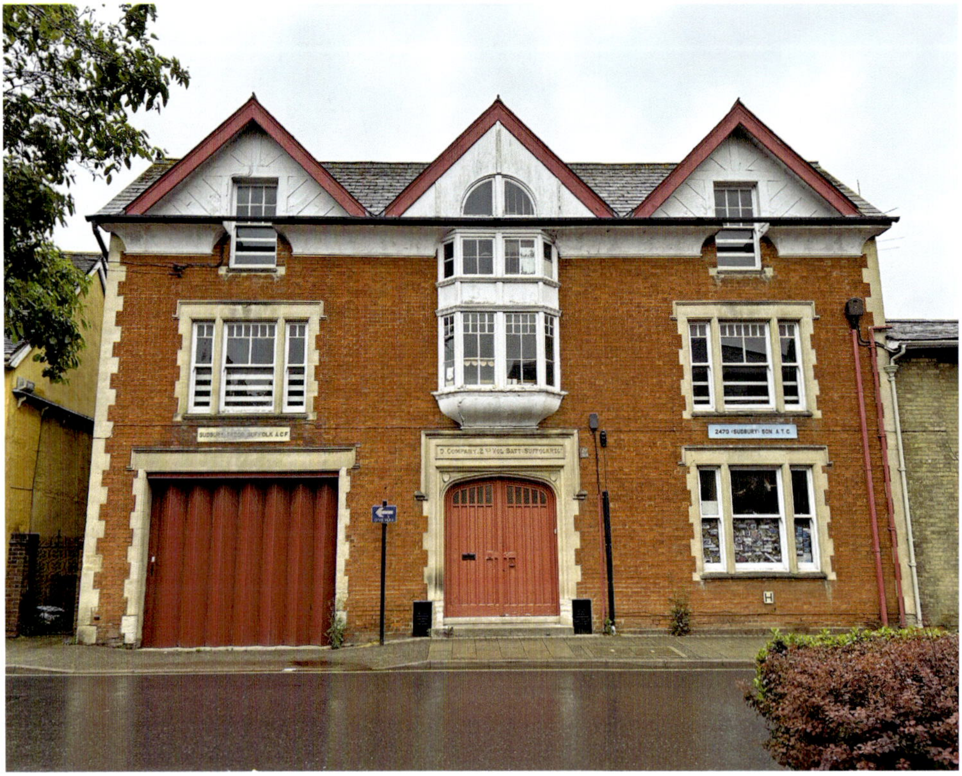

Drill Hall on Gainsborough Street, Sudbury, now used by the Air Training Corps and Army Cadet Force. Former home to the HQ 11th Suffolk Rifle Corps, West Suffolk (6th) Rifle Volunteers, and 2nd Volunteer Battalion Suffolk Regiment.

The Suffolk Militia was not the only part-time army that was raised in Suffolk. During the late eighteenth century Suffolk formed the first troops of mounted militia, known as Yeomanry Cavalry. The Suffolk Yeomanry was formed in 1794 when the persistent threat of invasion by France became a distinct possibility; this was considered not only an invasion of military force but also of social idealism. As home defences were being left to militiamen who were drawn predominantly from the working or labouring classes, the government established a new home defence force of volunteers drawn from higher up the socio-economic ladder, such as landowners and property owners. The Yeomanry would not only be used for home defence from foreign invasion, but also be a reliable force in the event of civil unrest. Initially five troops were formed, and this was expanded to nine troops by 1803. In 1828, like many other Yeomanry units, the Suffolk Yeomanry was disbanded, only to be reformed in 1831 and in 1883 it would acquire its distinctive name of 'The Loyal Suffolk Hussars'. In 1899, after a series of disastrous British defeats during the Second Anglo-Boer War, it was decided to test Yeomanry forces in overseas combat.

A renewed threat of invasion from the French during the mid-nineteenth century led to a reassessment of the country's home defences. With regular forces fighting in the Crimea and many others on garrison duty across the empire, a new part-time volunteer

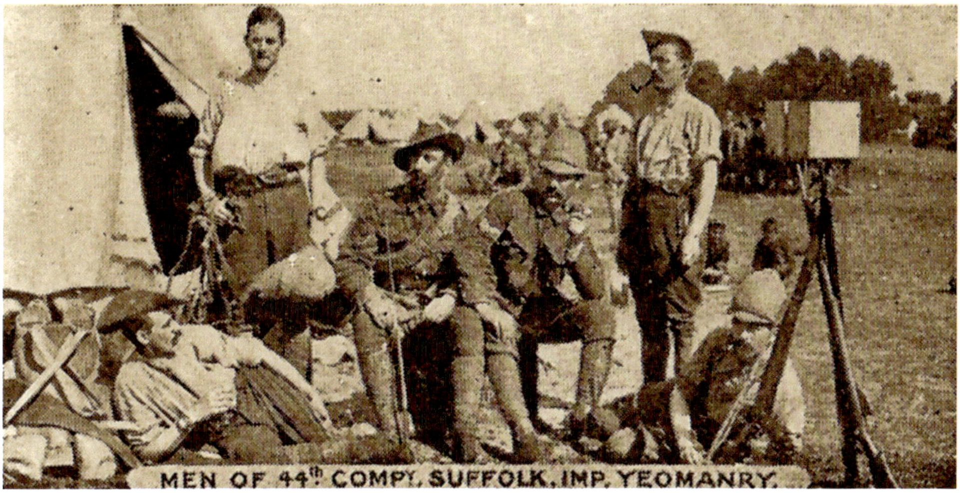

Soldiers of the 44th Company (Suffolk) Imperial Yeomanry in South Africa, one of two Suffolk Yeomanry battalions that served during the Boer War.

force was formed in 1859 to bolster the thinning home defences. Numerous Volunteer Rifle Corps were established across Suffolk, with a Volunteer Artillery Corps at Ipswich to defend its shoreline. Similar to the Yeomanry, the Suffolk Volunteer Rifles were filled with those from a different social status to the militia. While the militia tended to have a strict social divide, with upper-class men holding commissions and the working classes filling the ranks, the Volunteers tended to be middle-class men. This was primarily due to the financial constraints involved in joining a Volunteer Rifle Corps, such as men having to pay for their own uniform, equipment, rifle and ammunition. The Suffolk Rifle Volunteers became part of the Suffolk Regiment in 1881, and many of them saw active service overseas during the Boer War by forming Volunteer Companies which joined the Suffolk Regiment's regular battalions. The 1907 Territorial and Reserves Act that reorganised the county's militia also converted the Volunteer Rifle Corps into Territorial Force (TF) Battalions, Suffolk Regiment. The 4th (TF) Battalion was based at Ipswich, the 5th (TF) Battalion at Gibraltar Barracks in Bury St Edmunds, and a 6th (Cyclist) Battalion was also based at Ipswich in 1910. During the First World War, ten TF Battalions were raised, with the 4th serving in France and 5th in Gallipoli, Egypt and Palestine. By the end of the war, the Suffolk Yeomanry had been converted to dismounted infantry and formed the 15th (Yeomanry) Battalion, Suffolk Regiment. They served overseas in Egypt, Palestine and France. In 1921, Territorial Force units became known as the Territorial Army and once again served overseas during the Second World War, with the 4th and 5th Battalion attached to the ill-fated 18th Division. The 5th Battalion, which had been disbanded during the interwar years, had been reformed when the 4th Battalion was split to help strengthen the Territorial Army when war seemed imminent in 1939. Both Battalions were present during the fall of Singapore to the Japanese in February 1942, and spent the remainder of the war as prisoners. Many were forced to construct the infamous Burma-Thailand Railway. In 1940, following the Dunkirk evacuation, the 7th Battalion

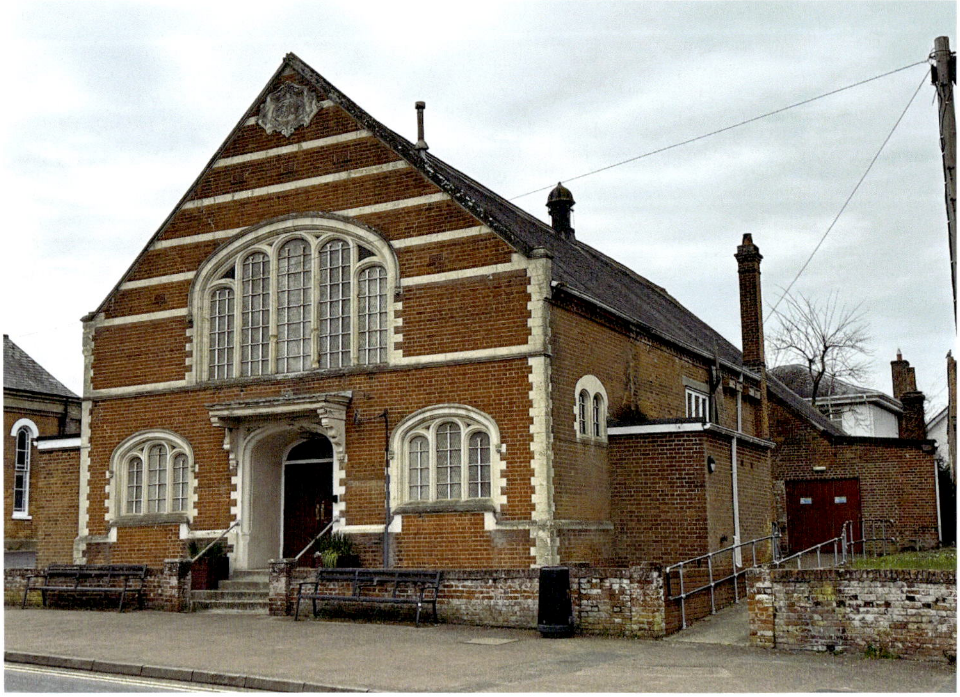

Rifle Hall on London Road, Halesworth. Originally built as a theatre in 1792, it would later be used as a Drill Hall by the 1st Volunteer Battalion Suffolk Regiment.

was formed for home defence; however by 1941 – after the initial threat of invasion had passed – the Battalion was converted to a Royal Armoured Corps unit. They would fight in the Tunisa Campaign in 1943, and then in Italy where they fought their way through the country to the Austrian border by the end of war and were subsequently disbanded. Throughout the two world wars, the Suffolk Regiment amassed over eighty battle honours, with the regular, territorial and yeomanry Battalions all contributing. After the war, the 5th Battalion was once again disbanded, leaving the Regiment with only one Territorial Battalion.

In 1920, all but fourteen of the most senior yeomanry regiments were converted in artillery units, with the Loyal Suffolk Hussars becoming part of the 108th (Suffolk & Norfolk) Field Brigade of the Royal Artillery (RA). Prior to the outbreak of the Second World War, the 108th Field Brigade was converted to the 55th (Suffolk & Norfolk Yeomanry) Anti-Tank Regiment, RA. In 1939, the unit was split to form the 55th (Suffolk Yeomanry) and the 65th (Norfolk Yeomanry) Anti-Tank Regiment. The 55th Regiment deployed to France in June 1944, supporting the 49th Division's infantry with their six- and seventeen-pounder guns during the North-West Europe campaign. In 1961 the 'Suffolk Yeomanry' once again merged to form the 308th (Suffolk and Norfolk Yeomanry) Field Regiment, RA. In 2006, the regiment had a new role to play in the British Army when it became No. 677 (Suffolk & Norfolk Yeomanry) Squadron of the Army Air Corps, a role which it continues to serve today, providing ground support to Apache helicopters.

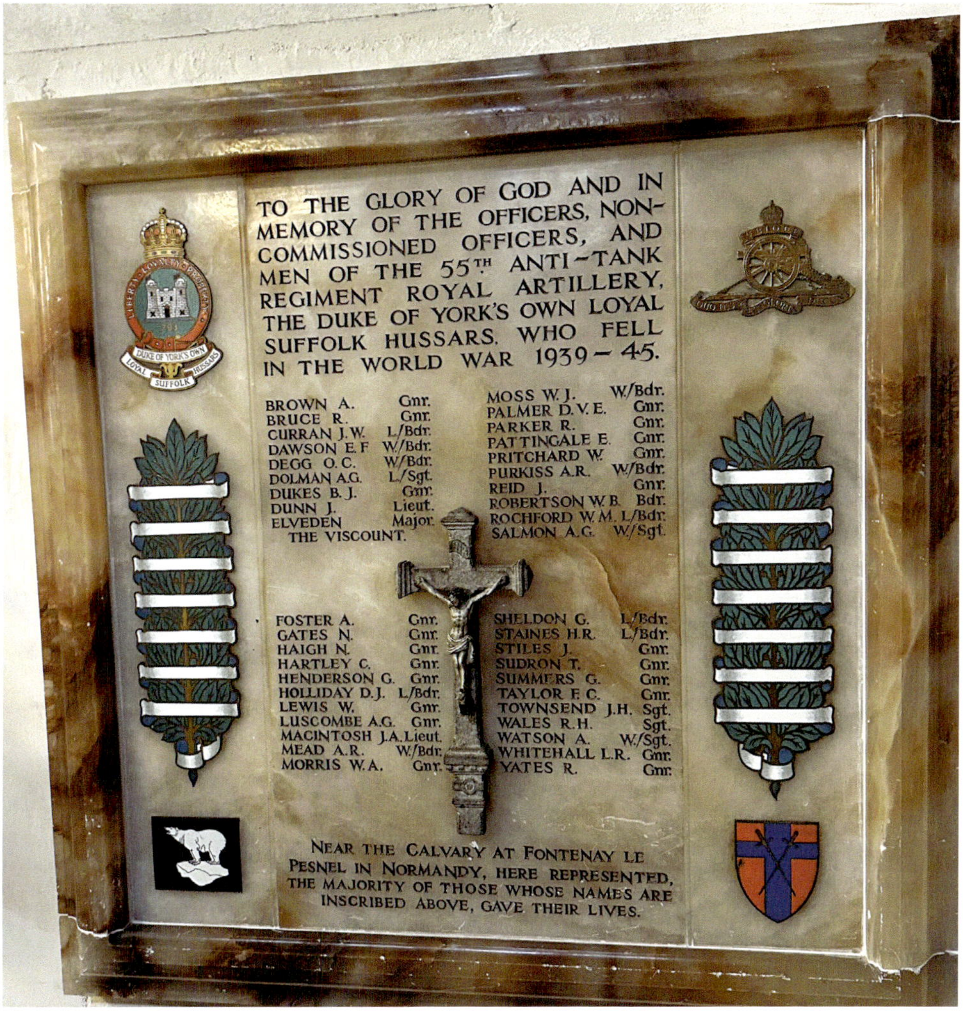

Memorial for those whose served with the 55th Anti-Tank Battalion, Suffolk Regiment, during the Second World War.

The World Wars to Present Day

The highest proportion of surviving physical military heritage found in Suffolk is, by far, associated to the two world wars. While the subject of this chapter could easily fill the pages of this book several times over, what has been included represents a mere sample of what the county has to offer. Where possible, these conflicts have also been discussed further in the chapters that follow.

The First World War

When war was declared against Germany in August 1914, a wave of patriotic enthusiasm saw men across Suffolk volunteer for military service. Recruits marched to railway stations with bands playing and crowds cheering, but many never returned home. Temporary camps were established to accommodate troops and provide additional training before leaving for the Western Front. However, it was not just troops who mustered in Suffolk during the early stage of the war. On the morning of Thursday 15 October 1914, over twelve crowded fishing trawlers from Ostend arrived at Lowestoft's North Quay, their passengers being Belgian refugees fleeing German occupation. Scantily dressed, their arduous journey across the North Sea took over thirty hours and many of the passengers (predominantly women and children) were found to be suffering from exposure. Tragically, a three-month-old child had died from inflammation of the lungs (accelerated by exposure) just before the port was reached. Similar stories came from Southwold Harbour; in both towns, Suffolk's dignitaries and common folk offered whatever help they could provide. The Home Office insisted the refugees proceed to London on special trains: fearing German spies could be hiding amongst them, the authorities wanted them settled away from the east coast.

While Suffolk temporarily housed military units and refugees, it became a longer-term temporary home for members of the No. 126 Company, Canadian Forestry Corps (CFC). Under the command of Major A. B. R. Kenny, they moved their Company Headquarters in September 1918 from Ampthill, Bedfordshire, to Downham Hall at Santon Downham. However, the Company's activities on the Downham estate predate this move. There was an unprecedented demand of timber during the First World War, as wood was needed in all aspects of military life and was required across a vast geographical area. With so many men called up for military service, the British government requested help from Canada's specialists to help keep up with the demand for timber. By this time, they had produced approximately 70 per cent of all the Allies' timber. In November 1918, a light railway line was constructed to transport felled logs to the sawmill near Santon Downham, with the Great Eastern Railway main line that ran to the north of the River Little Ouse, and felling sites at High Lodge to the south of the Company's headquarters. The Downham estate was acquired by the Forestry Commission, now Forestry England, in 1924.

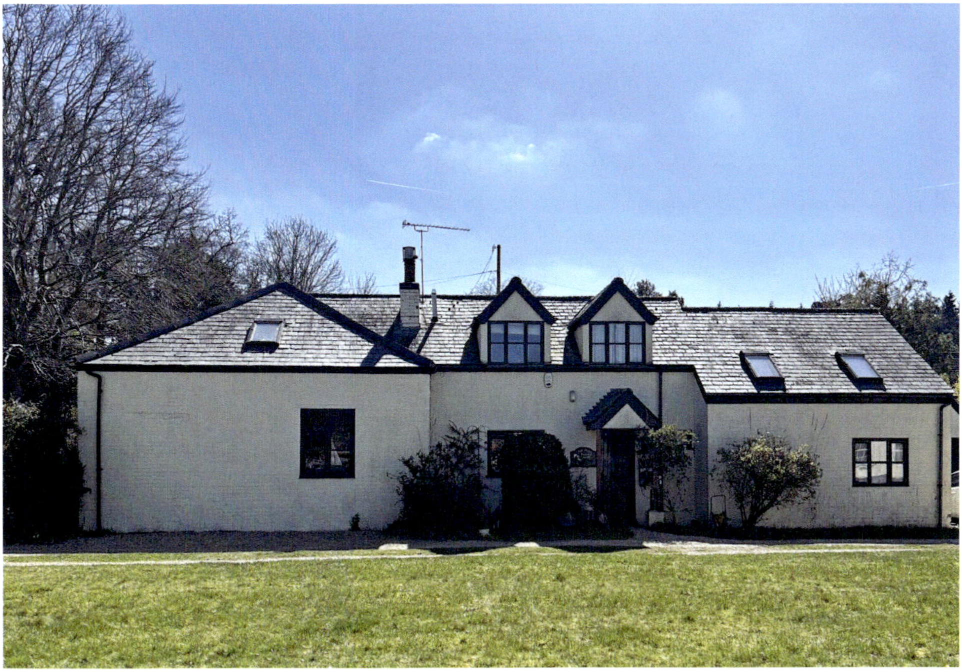

Downham Hall itself was demolished in the late 1920s, with only the billiards room (pictured) and icehouse remaining to the south. The coach house to the west and tack room to the north were converted into private residences.

During the course of the war, private residences where either freely given over to be used for temporary military functions or forcefully requisitioned by the government. In 1914, the British Red Cross and the Order of St John of Jerusalem combined to form the Joint War Committee, pooling their resources to establish auxiliary hospitals. Throughout Suffolk, all manner of buildings were converted into auxiliary hospitals, from small private homes and community centres to schools and stately homes. Auxiliary hospitals tended to care for patients with injuries and illnesses that weren't considered life threatening. The buildings were significantly less crowded and strict than military hospitals, so patients could feel more at ease while they convalesced. Like many of the hospitals in Suffolk, Ampton Hall treated sick and wounded British soldiers and those of her allies too. One of the earliest British soldiers to die at Ampton was Second Anglo-Boer War veteran Private Alfred Green, who died of his wounds in 1914. Several Canadian and Australian soldiers also died while receiving treatment at Ampton Hall, such as Private Rupert Duffham Bussell from Quirindi, New South Wales, who enlisted with the Australian Imperial Force in August 1915 and entered the front-line trenches for the first time on 12 July 1916, fighting at Fromelles the following week which resulted in devastating losses for the 56th Battalion. Bussell was wounded in action on 20 July 1916 after receiving a severe gunshot wound to his head. Admitted to Ampton Hall Hospital on 22 July, Private Bussell died three days later. Like many soldiers who fought during the First World War, Bussell would not return home to his family. However, unlike those who fell on the battlefield and have no known grave, Bussell was buried in the St Bartholomew churchyard in the neighbouring village of Ingham. Another patient from overseas was Sergeant Donald McLean, from Marta Township, Ontario, Canada, who was wounded by shrapnel at Passchendaele on 3 November 1917, requiring his foot to be amputated on 27 November 1917 and died of his wounds on 1 November 1918. Initially buried in the churchyard in Ingham, his remains were repatriated in June 1919 and buried in his family plot in Orillia, Ontario.

Suffolk also played host to some unexpected guests. The day after Britain entered the war on 4 August 1914, a trawler off the coast of Harwich noticed a ship suspiciously throwing objects overboard. HMS *Amphion*, a Royal Navy cruiser assigned to the Harwich Flotilla, led destroyers of the 3rd Flotilla to investigate. They discovered the German minelayer, the SMS *Konigin Luise* – disguised with the colours of a Great Eastern Railway steamship – so the Flotilla gave chase and sunk the minelayer. Carrying rescued German sailors, the Flotilla was returning to Harwich in the early hours of 6 August when, with devastating effect, HMS *Amphion* struck a mine the *Konigin Luise* had deployed earlier. Several British crew and one German sailor were killed, but the rest of the survivors were picked up by the accompanying destroyers. The surviving German sailors were transported to Shotley Naval Hospital and ultimately became the first German prisoners of war (POW) in Britain.

Not all the unexpected guests were kept in Suffolk against their will; in fact over 1,000 Russian soldiers had been brought from POW camps in Germany to Exning in late 1918 to receive training to fight the communist 'Red Army' in post-revolution Russia. These soldiers were to form part of the Russian 'White Army': those who were loyal to Tsar

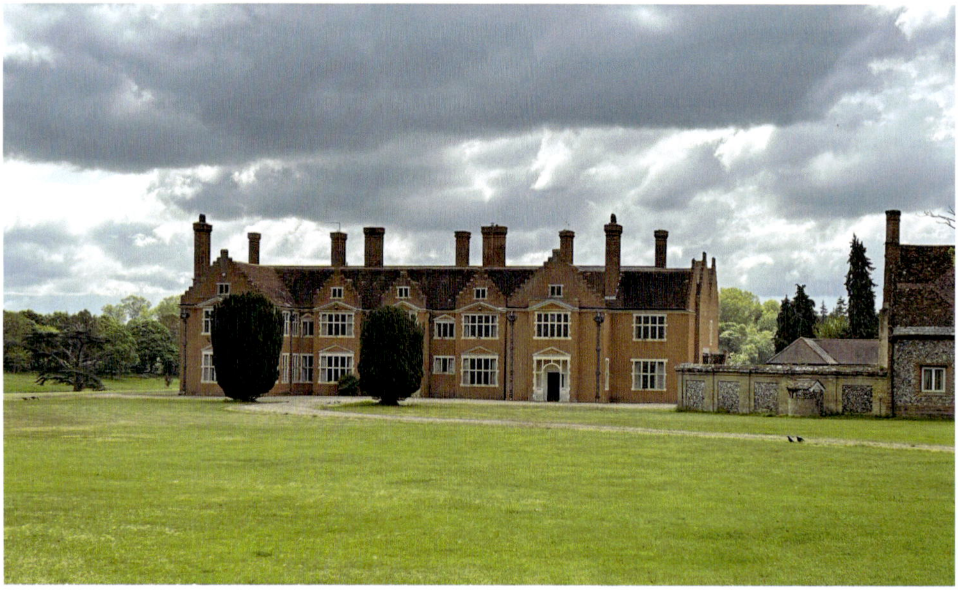

Ampton Hall. Serving as a Red Cross Hospital from 16 October 1914 to 31 January 1919, some 6,568 sick and wounded soldiers were cared for by the staff at Ampton Hall.

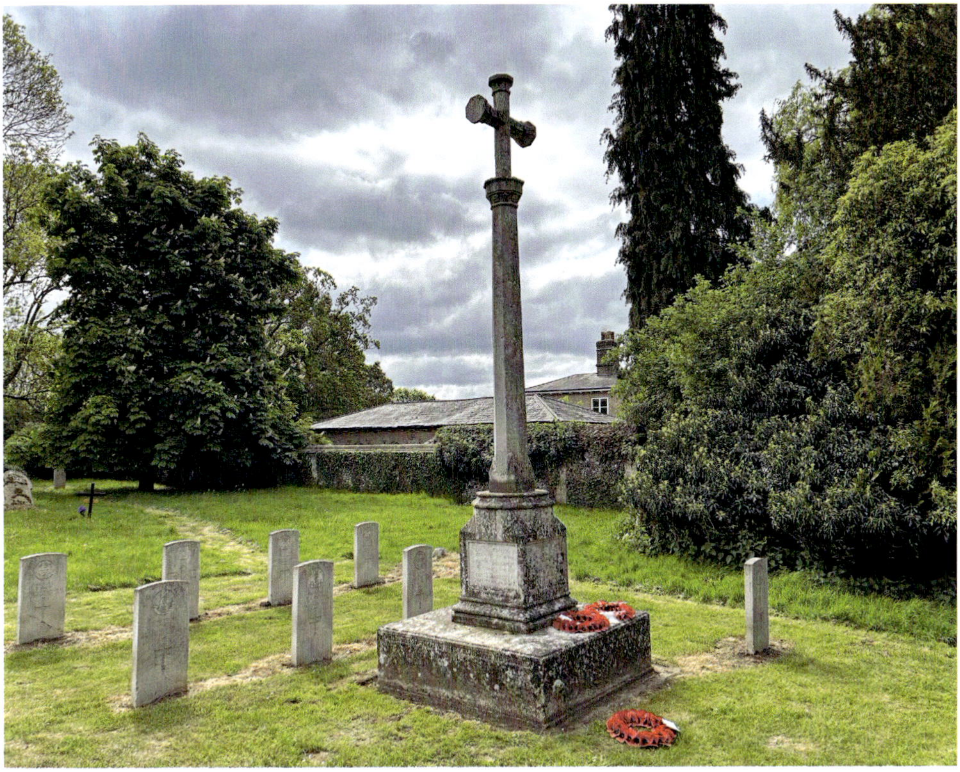

Private Bussell's grave along with other patients of Ampton Hall who would be buried at St Bartholomew's churchyard, Ingham. Forty patients would succumb to their injuries and illnesses.

Nicholas II, who had been executed in 1918 after the Bolshevik Red Army seized control in 1917. The White Army received support from former allies of Tsarist Russia, including Britain, France and the US, and received training in the latest weapons and tactics while at the Exning camp. Ultimately the war was lost and two soldiers of the Imperial Russian Army – Lieutenant Eugene Petrov and Lieutenant Nicholas De Meder – died during the time in Suffolk and are buried in Exning cemetery.

As the war progressed, new technologies were introduced onto the battlefield, having been tested in secret in Suffolk. Elveden Hall and its expansive grounds, located 10 miles north of Bury St Edmunds, was chosen for its remote location to test Britain's first armoured tanks. Inspired by the use of armoured trains during the Second Anglo-Boer War, it was hoped that tanks would help break the deadlock on the Western Front. The prototype called 'Little Willie' (named after the Crown Prince Wilhelm of Germany) was designed by Lieutenant Walter Wilson, Royal Naval Air Service, and William Tritton, the Managing Director of William Foster & Co. of Lincoln, where the new weapon was built in late 1915. In early 1916, its successor came, which was known as 'Mother' (although also known as 'Big Willie'); this became the model for the Mark I tanks used during the latter part of the war. After they were built in Lincoln, the tanks were transported in secrecy to Elveden in spring 1916. Those building them believed them to be water

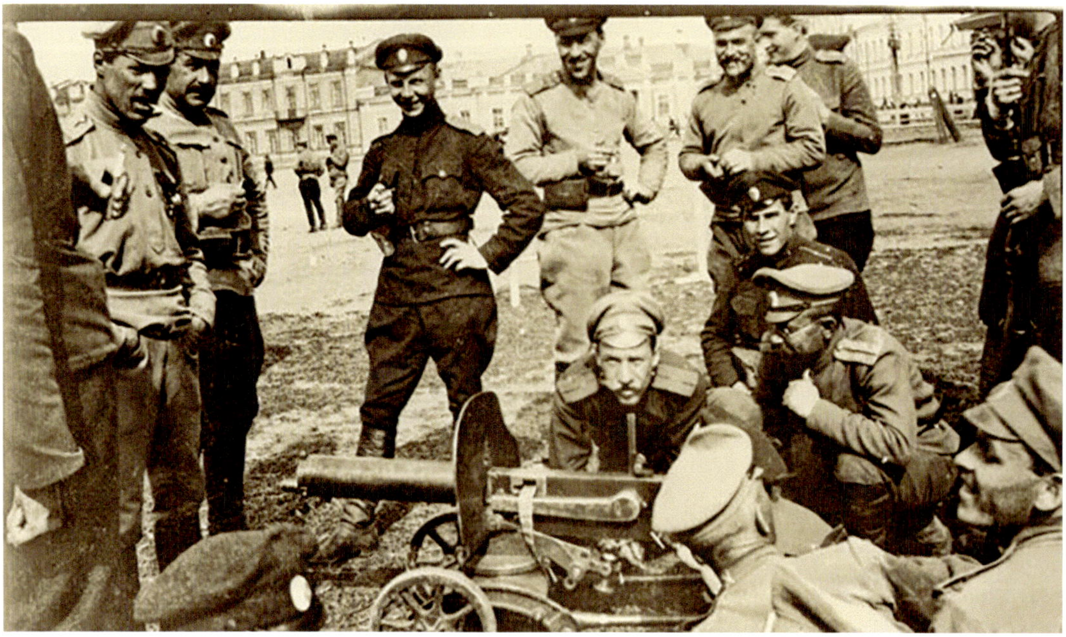

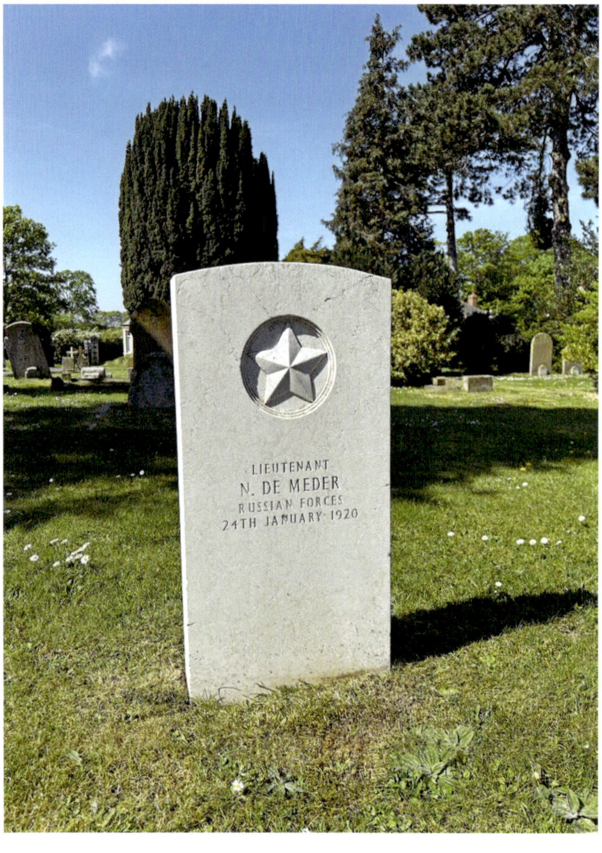

Above: Russian 'White Army' officers receiving training in the use of a Russian Maxim machine gun. (Australian War Memorial)

Left: Grave of Lieutenant De Meder, Russian Forces. De Meder took his own life using a revolver on 24 January 1920.

tanks, so they referred to them as 'Tanks'. Once at Elveden, the vast estate was used to recreate the battlefields of the Western Front, to test the tanks and their crew on the terrain they would face overseas. After King George V inspected the tanks at Elveden on 26 July 1916, General Haig decided that the first tanks were to be sent to France to assist in the Somme Offensive. Forty-nine tanks were to join the attack on the village of Flers-Courcelette on 15 September 1916, however many broke down before reaching the front line. Although only fifteen entered the battle, they struck fear into the Bavarian troops they encountered.

While not entirely a new technology, the role of military aircraft for reconnaissance was refined during First World War. Research and testing sites were established in Suffolk as a new type of warfare was introduced: aerial combat. At the outbreak of the war in 1914, the Royal Naval Air Service (RNAS) quickly learned the value of flying boats in marine reconnaissance. A naval air base at Felixstowe had been commissioned in August 1913, with the RNAS being formed in July the following year. RNAS Felixstowe became one the most important east coast flying boat stations; being positioned directly opposite U-boat bases across the North Sea it would become the largest seaplane base in the UK during the First World War. Felixstowe became the centre of seaplane design, including experimenting with various methods of launching and retrieval of seaplanes from naval vessels. On 1 April 1918, the RNAS and Royal Flying Corps (RFC) merged to form the Royal Air Force (RAF), and the air station at Felixstowe became the Seaplane Experimental Station, renamed the Marine Aircraft Experimental Establishment in 1924. The air station closed in 1962 and is now the site of a container port.

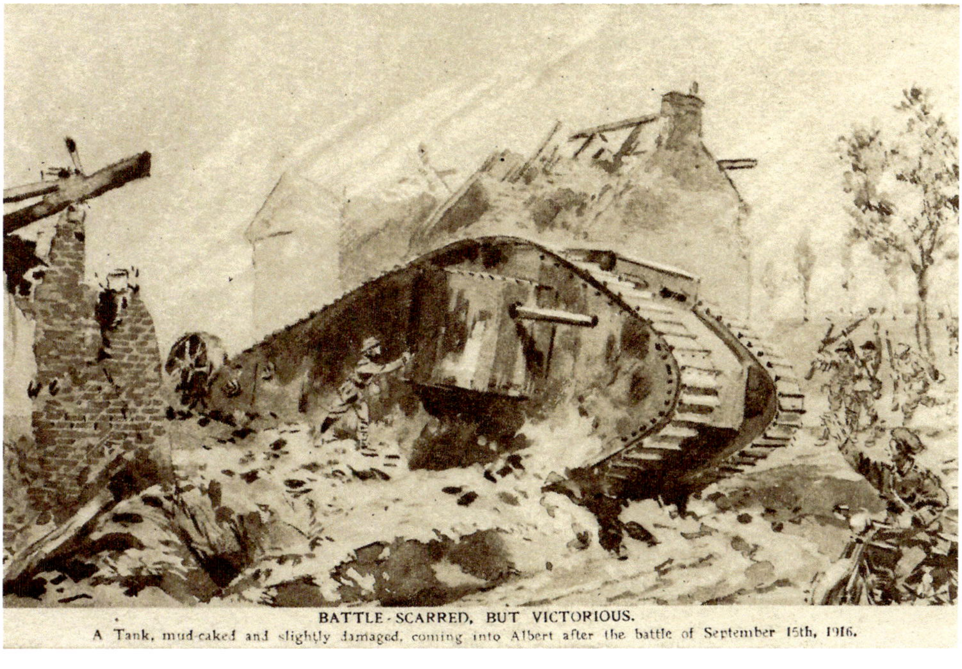

Artist's impression of the first tank attack on the village of Flers-Courcelette on 15 September 1916.

The RFC established the Central Flying School (CFS) in 1912, and in 1915 the CFS created the Armament Experimental Flight (AEF), which was to be based at Orford Ness because of its remote and inaccessible location. The First World War would start a long history of secretive military experimentation carried out at Orford Ness. In 1915, an area of King's Marsh was drained and levelled to create an airfield, and it received its first aircraft soon after. Here they carried out research on the aerial use of machine guns, bombs, sights, incendiary bullets for use against zeppelins, and navigational equipment. As the RFC's experimental flight and armaments sections needed to work closely together, the Aircraft Testing Flight (ATF) relocated from Upavon to Martlesham Heath to be nearer the AEF. In late 1916, the AEF and ATF combined at Martlesham Heath to become the Aeroplane Experimental Station, renamed the Aeroplane and Armament Experimental Establishment (A&AEE) in 1924. They tested armament and equipment that would be later used during the Second World War.

The RFC's involvement in Suffolk during the First World War wasn't limited to flight and armament experimentation. In 1916, the Elmswell Aerodrome, located at Lea Farm between the villages of Elmswell and Great Ashfield, was assigned to No. 75 Home Defence (HD) Squadron, RFC. The unit's role would be to defend the East Anglian skies against German raids. The Squadron's Headquarters and 'C' Flight were stationed at Elmswell, while 'A' Flight was at Hadleigh Aerodrome and 'B' Flight at Harling Road Aerodrome in Norfolk. Their mission was to intercept Zeppelin raids, with the Squadron's first action against the enemy taking place on 24–25 September 1916. There were several other small airfields in Suffolk during the war, such as Hazelwood Aerodrome at Aldeburgh (first an RNAS Night Landing Ground then an RAF Anti-Submarine Patrol Observer's School), and the area to the west of Covehithe Broad, which was used as a night landing ground and acted as a satellite station for RNAS Great Yarmouth and used in anti-Zeppelin patrols.

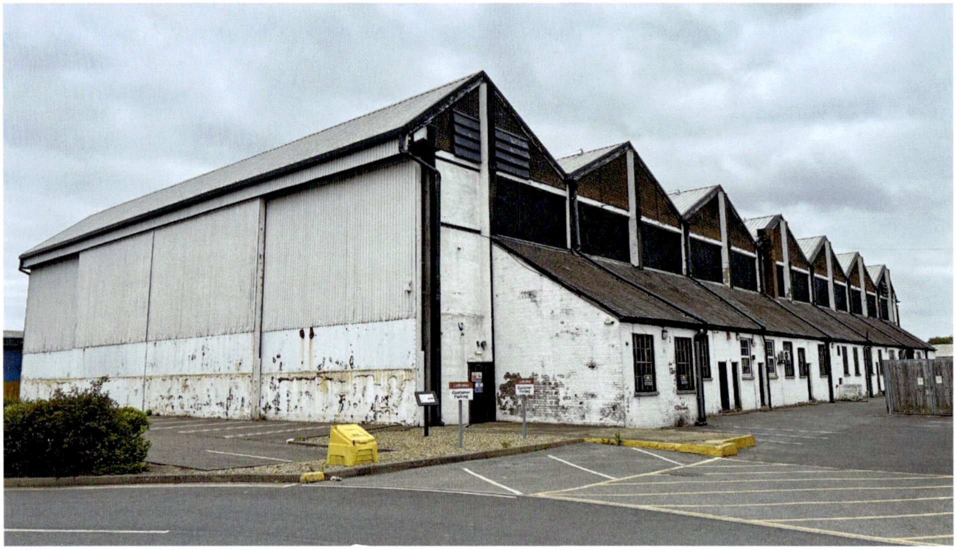

Designed in 1924, a former Type 'A' hangar at RAF Martlesham Heath.

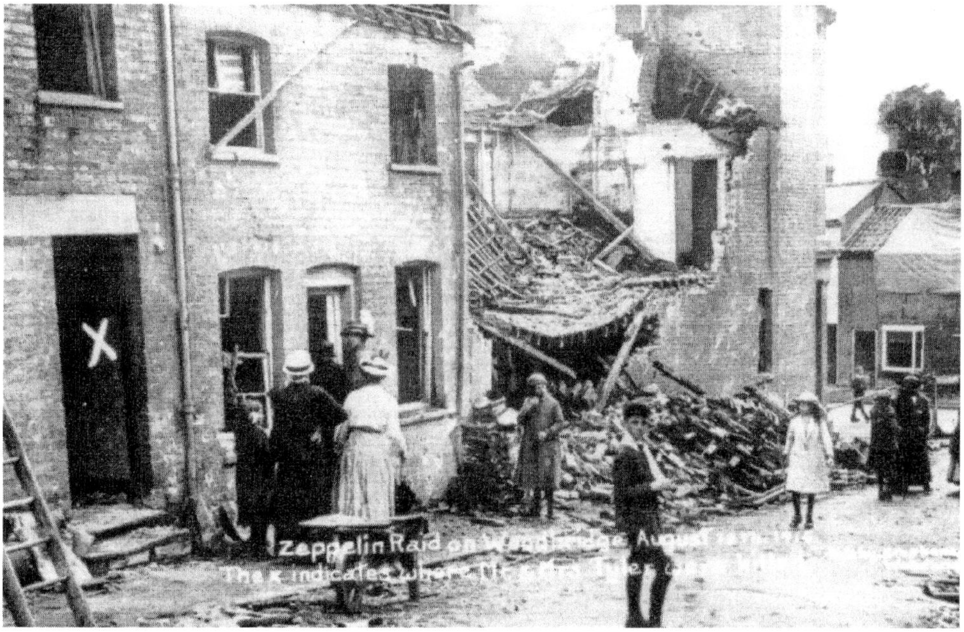

Damage caused by the Zeppelin L10 on Woodbridge on 12 August 1915. The 'X' on the image marks where Mr and Mrs Tyler were standing when they were killed during the attack on St John's Hill.

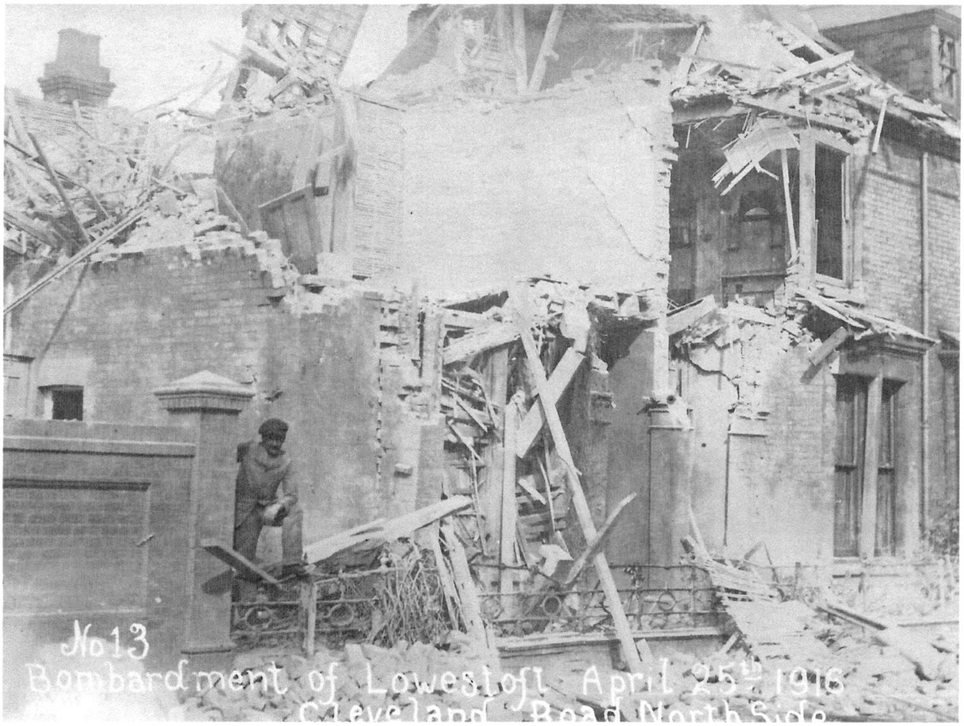

Destruction caused by the German naval bombardment of Lowestoft on 25 April 1916.

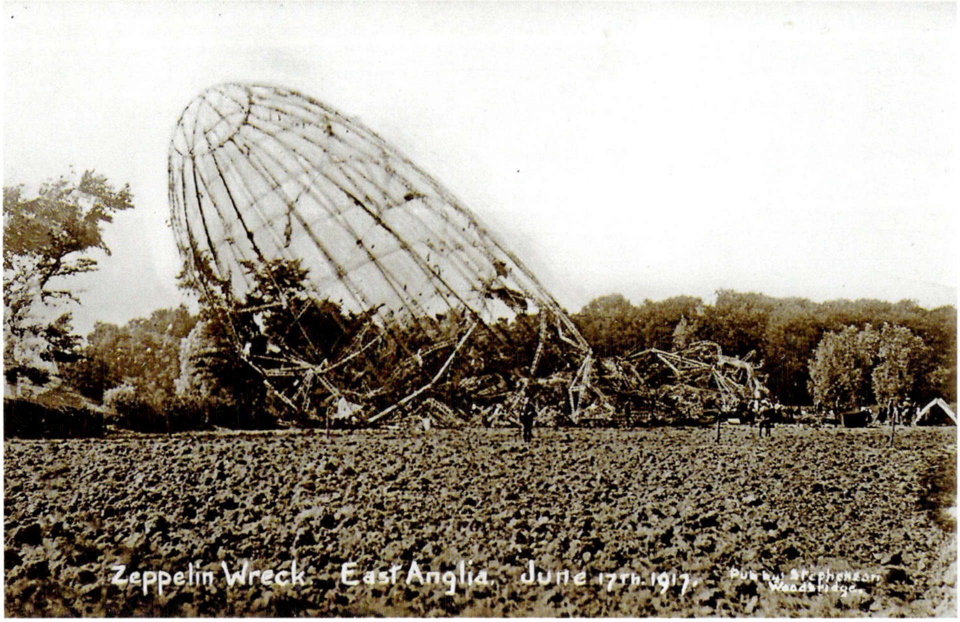

Scene of the downed Zeppelin at Theberton.

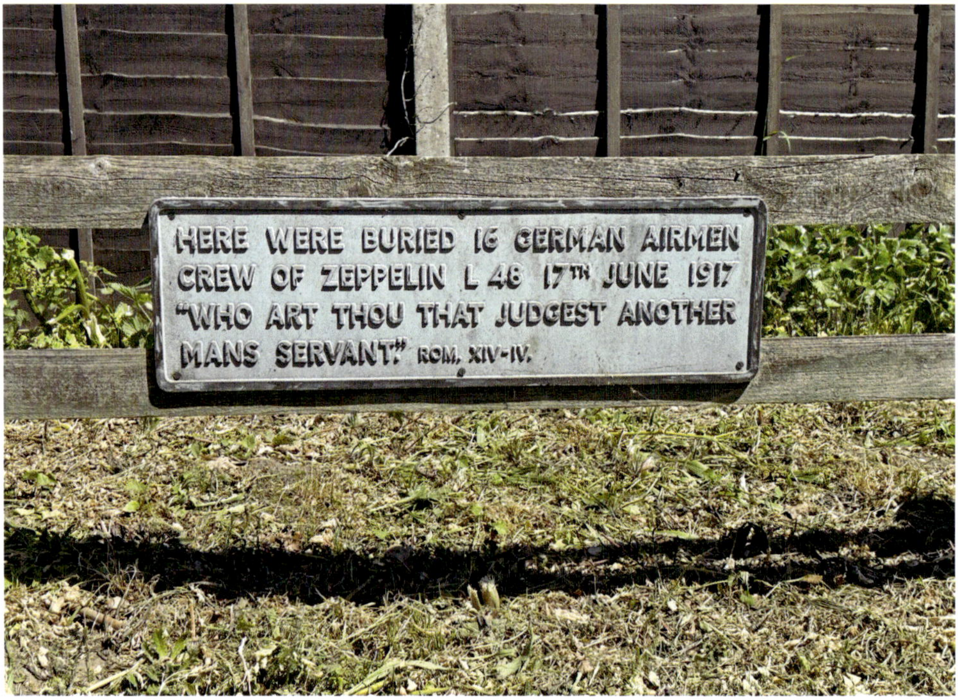

Three of the eighteen Zeppelin crew survived, with those who perished being buried in St Peter's churchyard, Theberton. They were later reinterred at the German Military Cemetery, Cannock Chase, Staffordshire.

Zeppelins first appeared over the night skies of Suffolk on 15–16 April 1915, causing fear among those who had previously thought themselves safe on their impregnable island. Passing over Southwold, the German Zeppelin L5 made its way to Lowestoft and dropped bombs that – thankfully – caused only limited damage at Halesworth and Reydon. In Lowestoft, properties were damaged by Zeppelin L11's raid on 9–10 August 1915, resulting in one fatality – eighteen-year-old Kate Crawford. The town would go on to suffer another Zeppelin raid later that year and be subjected to a naval bombardment on Easter Monday 1916. Many locals fled to the countryside out of fear of further attacks. Zeppelin attacks continued for the next two years, with bombs dropped over Felixstowe, Bury St Edmunds, Stowmarket, Sudbury and Woodbridge. By late 1917, the majority of Germany's Zeppelin fleet had been destroyed and their crews killed or captured. On 16–17 June 1917, Zeppelin L48 was intercepted by pilots from the RFC 37 Squadron over the coast of Great Yarmouth and, after a series of attacks, the pilots crippled the airship, sending it on a slow decent towards Leiston where it became engulfed in flames as it crashed near Theberton.

The Second World War

Suffolk performed no less an important role in the Second World War than it had in the previous global conflict. The county's earliest involvement began similarly to the First World War, however this time Suffolk became involved before Britain had even declared war, by providing a safe harbour for the displaced. In the early months of the war, children began to arrive in Suffolk as it was feared that large cities and industrial areas would be subjected to enemy attacks, with an article in the *Evening News* on 1 September 1939 reporting that evacuated children had arrived by pleasure ships at Lowestoft and Felixstowe. This period would be known as the 'Phoney War' as the attacks failed to materialise and many of the evacuated children returned home. There were, however, children arriving in Suffolk prior to these evacuations. From 1938, thousands of German children, many of whom were Jewish, arrived at Harwich to escape Nazi persecution. Known as the 'Kindertransport', this series of rescue efforts resulted in over 10,000 children arriving in Great Britain between December 1938 and May 1940. Arriving at Lowestoft Central Station in December 1938, 520 children were transported to their accommodation at Pakefield Holiday Camp (now Pontin's Pakefield Holiday Village) and the St Felix School, Reydon.

Throughout the war people under German occupation would attempt to reach the safety of neutral or allied nations, with a journey to Britain offering the best chance of success for many in western Europe. On 21 September 1941, two Dutchmen arrived at Sizewell beach having paddled for fifty-six hours from the Netherlands in a kayak. They wanted not to only escape the German occupation, but to also join the Allied forces. The two Dutchmen – Henri and Willem Peteri – had heard of attempts by others who tried to escape the Nazi-occupied Netherlands using boats, however many of the escapees had been either captured or killed. When they learned of people from Scandinavia reaching Britain by canoe, they decided that by using a smaller craft their attempt may remain undetected. They purchased a (somewhat ironically) German-made kayak in Rotterdam and left after nightfall on 19 September 1941. Upon arriving at Sizewell beach, they were met by a local uniformed policeman and were taken to the police station in Leiston. After being interviewed and released from custody, Henri and his brother would make their way to London, as the Dutch military's headquarters was operating from there. Henri would go on to serve as an officer with the Dutch Marines for the remainder of the war, while Willem would join the Royal Dutch Navy. Unfortunately, Willem would become a POW in October 1942 and would remain at the German camp near Lubeck for the rest of the war. Thirty-two people attempted the journey to England by kayak during the war, with eight surviving the crossing, and only three surviving until the end of the war.

Of all the physical military heritage associated with the Second World War, none is more prominent and widely dispersed across the county than that associated with the defence against invasion. Following the evacuation of the BEF from Dunkirk in May 1940, invasion by German forces was deemed a serious threat. In preparation, General Edmund Ironside (Commander in Chief of Home Forces) devised a series of coastal and inland defences in areas considered to be vulnerable to enemy invasion, such as the low-lying land and stretches of gentle gradient beach in Suffolk. Inland, 'Stop-Lines' were a series of pillboxes, barbed wire and anti-tank ditches that crisscrossed the country and were built in the hope to stop, or at the very least, delay the enemy's advance. Seven stop-lines passed through Suffolk, covering approximately 225 miles of defences and included some 300 pillboxes. The most heavily fortified, accounting for 118 of these pillboxes and completed by August 1940, was 'Line C'. This was known as the 'Corp Line' from September 1940, and it started in Colchester in Essex, entered Suffolk at Bures, and ran north through the east of Suffolk, including Sudbury, Lavenham, Bury St Edmunds and Mildenhall, then travelled west and joined the Great Ouse river. Inland defences also included fortified 'nodal points': larger villages and towns where four or five major roads converged, or where there was a major river crossing. Along the 'Corp Line', the nodal points included Mildenhall, Bury St Edmunds, Lond Melford and Sudbury. Thankfully none of these defences were ever needed; had they been needed it would have been down to the Suffolk Home Guard to man them, along with reserves from regular units manning the coastal defences.

In the event of a successful invasion, Churchill was determined to ensure that their advance would with be a fraught affair. Auxiliary Units, more commonly known as 'Stay Behinds', would go to ground if an invasion took place, and conduct guerrilla warfare-style attacks on the enemy behind their own lines. Throughout Suffolk, Auxiliary Units trained for such an eventuality. To assist with the Units' activities, the Special Duties Section (SDS) was created and tasked with observing and reporting on the activities of the German invaders. This information would be transmitted from 'OUT' Stations to radio operators using a secret, lightweight, short-range radio transceiver ('TRD') at an 'IN' Station. In the village of Hundon the SDS Auxiliary Unit (Signals) requisitioned the country house Bachelor's Hall, converting a barn in the grounds into a workshop to upgrade and maintain the TRDs. Using VHF with two-way open language messaging, it was believed that TRD communications could not be intercepted. First invented at the University of Cambridge in the early 1930s, it was developed further by the Secret Intelligence Service until Auxiliary Units (Signals) refined the technology to work in the field.

Mimicking the actions taken in 1914, across the county all types of buildings were requisitioned or offered to assist the war effort. In Long Melford, Kentwell Hall was

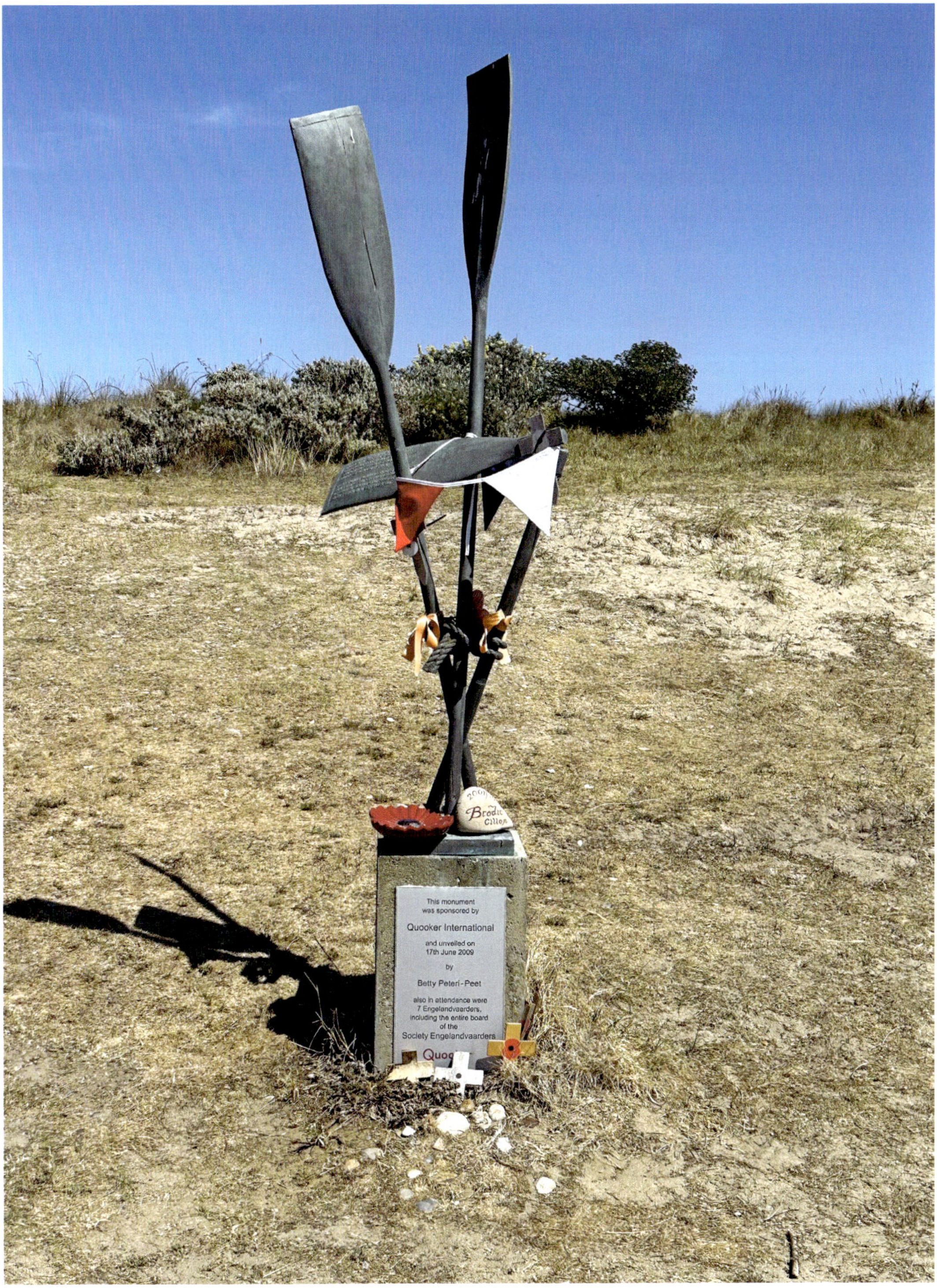

Memorial at Sizewell Beach. Featuring three paddles – one for each of the two brothers who survived the journey, and a broken paddle to remember the brother who did not.

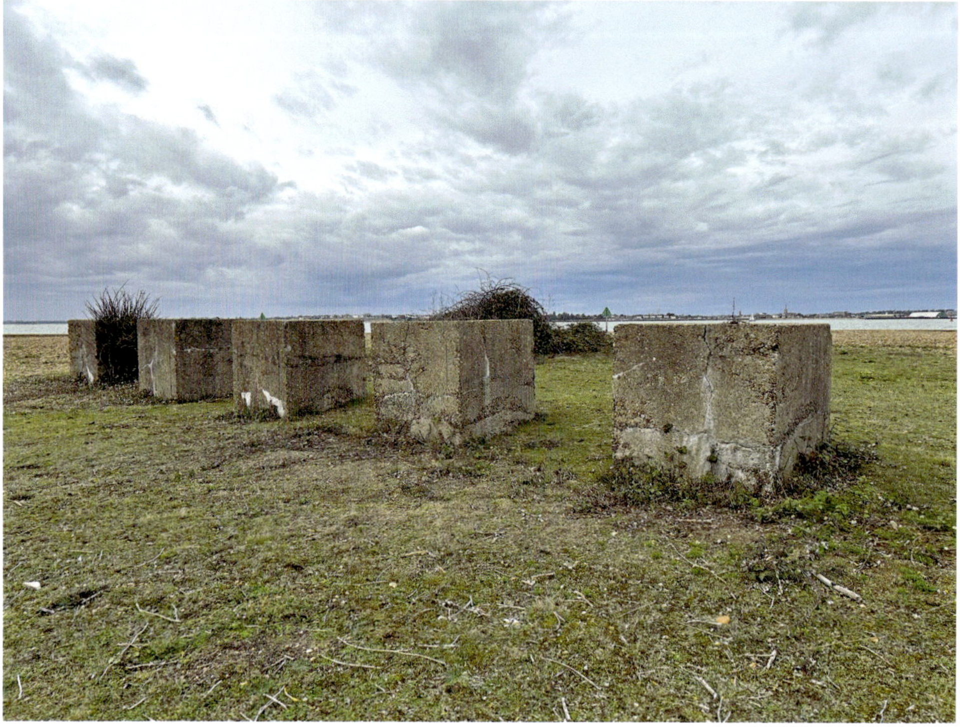

Anti-tank blocks near the Felixstowe coast.

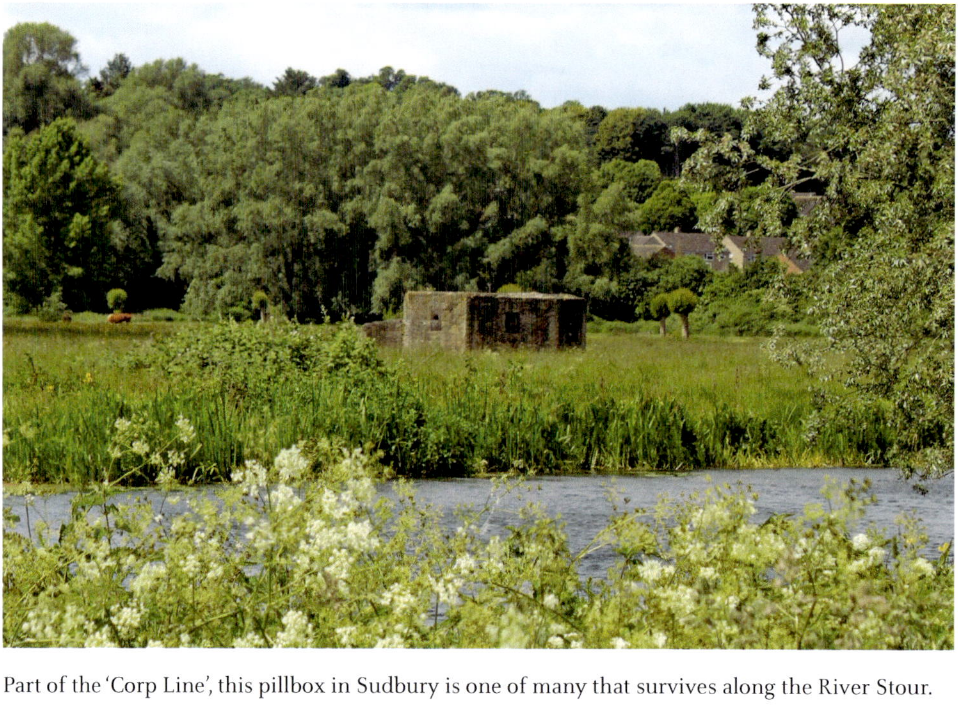

Part of the 'Corp Line', this pillbox in Sudbury is one of many that survives along the River Stour.

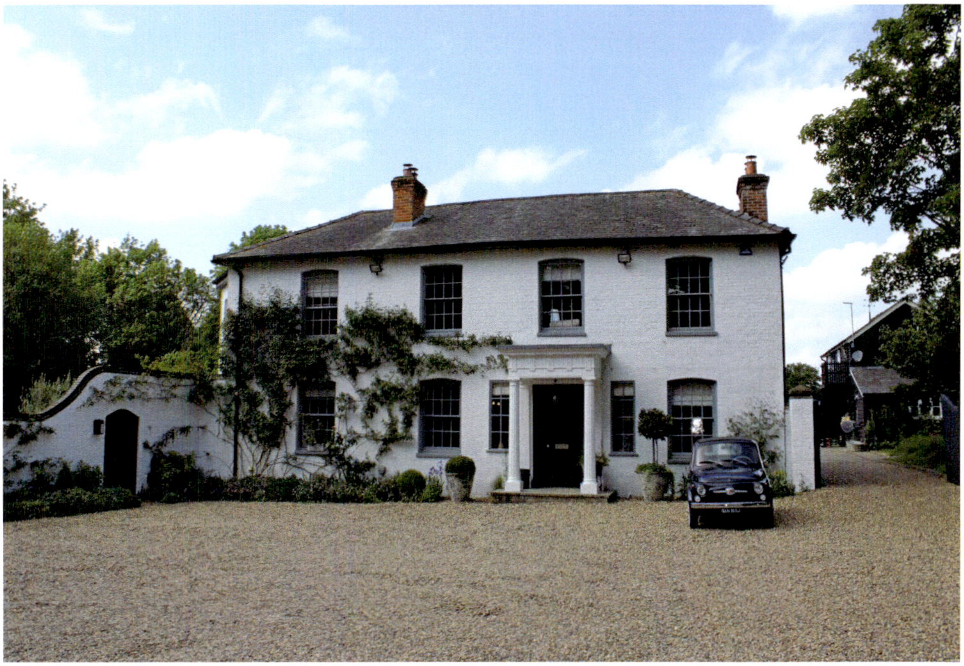

Bachelor's Hall, Hundon, home to the SDS Auxiliary Unit (Signals). The barn to the right was used as a workshop to upgrade and maintain the TRDs.

requisitioned for military use and Melford Hall was offered to the War Office at the outbreak of war in 1939. The expansive grounds were first used as a training camp, before being utilised as a transit camp for those being deployed to fight in Europe, with Nissen huts to house soldiers strewn across the grounds. In May 1944, the famous 'Desert Rats' of the 8th Army moved from Brandon to Orwell Park School, where they carried out waterproofing work on their tanks in preparation for D-Day. Not all military camps were set up in such opulent settings, however, such as the Culford Camps near Thetford. Here, a large contingent of new recruits of the Women's Timber Corps (WTC) were sent for a month's training, learning how to identify trees and measure woodland, then fell, haul and process standing timber. They were formed to replace the male forestry workers who had joined the Armed Forces and to reduce the reliance of imported timber. The WTC-produced timber would be used for tracks used during the D-Day landing, pit props for the mining industry, telegraph poles for communications, and they also processed beech that was needed to build Mosquito aircraft. At Bawdsey, near the mouth of the River Debden, the Air Ministry purchased Bawdsey Manor in 1936 to develop one of Britain's most important defence measures. Renamed RAF Bawdsey, it became a research station working on the development of radar; its position near the coast and the likely flight lines of German aircraft made it the perfect location for a Chain Home (CH) Radar site, as they could bounce radio beams off the enemy aircraft to detect them and track their trajectory.

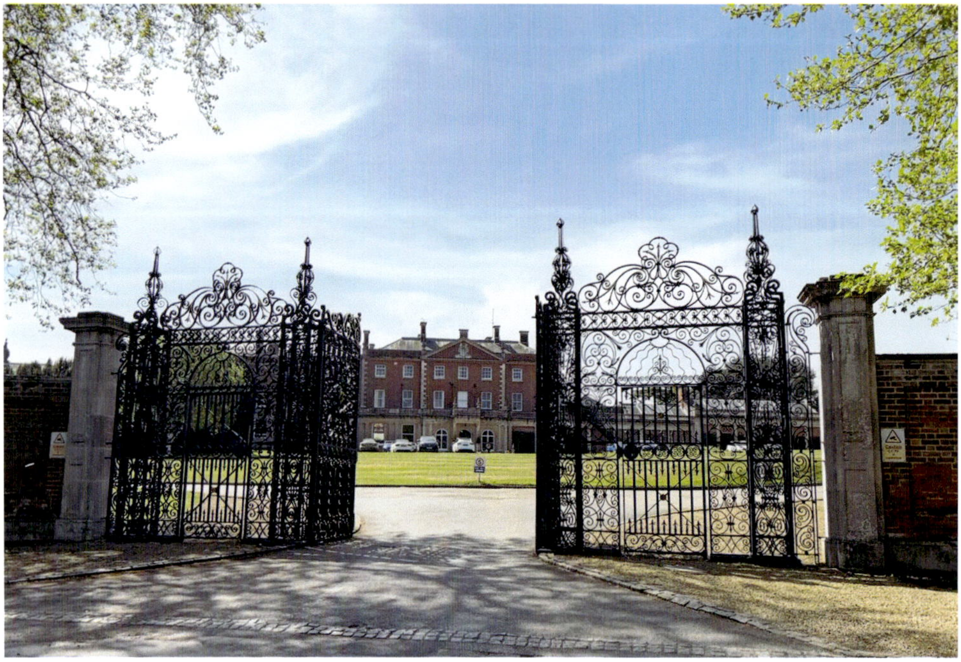

Orwell Park School hosted the Desert Rats as they prepared for D-Day.

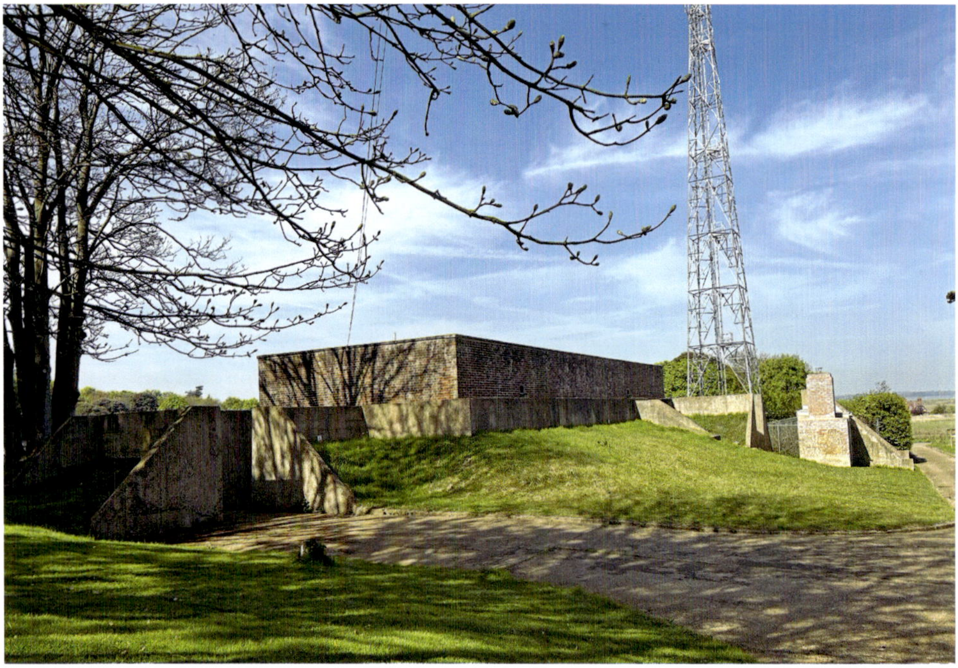

Former Transmitter Block at RAF Bawdsey. RAF Bawdsey would continue to be used as a training school and radar site until 1974. While Bawdsey Manor is now privately owned, the Second Word War Transmitter Block on the Bawdsey estate is now a museum and open to the public.

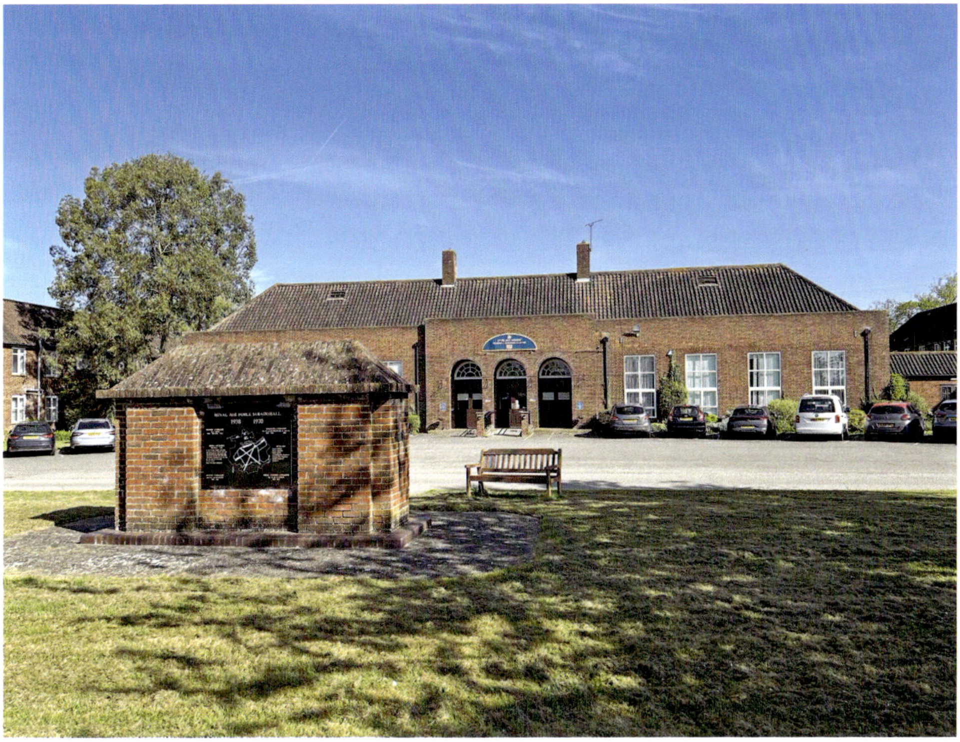

RAF Stradishall memorial, with Sterling House Training and Conference Centre in the background. Built in 1938, Sterling House was the quarters for flight officers stationed at RAF Stradishall during the Second World War.

It is not difficult to understand why Suffolk was considered an important part of what was known as 'bomber country'. In 1939, Suffolk already had RAF airfields at Mildenhall, Honington, Stradishall, Wattisham and Newmarket Heath, and had three more being built for Bomber Command. Some of these airfields would end up being reallocated to the United States Army Air Force (USAAF). From 1942, American service personnel began to arrive in Britain, with over 100,000 US airmen stationed in the country by early 1943. The largest concentration of American pilots, their crews and support personnel were in the east of England, and this would become affectionately known as the 'friendly invasion'. By early June 1944, over 70,000 Americans were posted to Suffolk airfields and various support facilities. During the war some twenty airfields were occupied by the USAAF, primarily by a Bombardment Group (BG) of the 8th USAAF. This included Station 468 at Bury St Edmunds (Rougham), which was home to over 3,000 American service personnel of the 94th BG and their Boeing B-17 Flying Fortresses. Here they received morale-boosting visits from musicians and Hollywood stars, such as Glenn Miller and Clark Gable. However, the 8th USAAF also had Fighter Groups flying from Martlesham Heath, and Wattisham, while fighters from the 8th and 9th USAAF flew from Raydon.

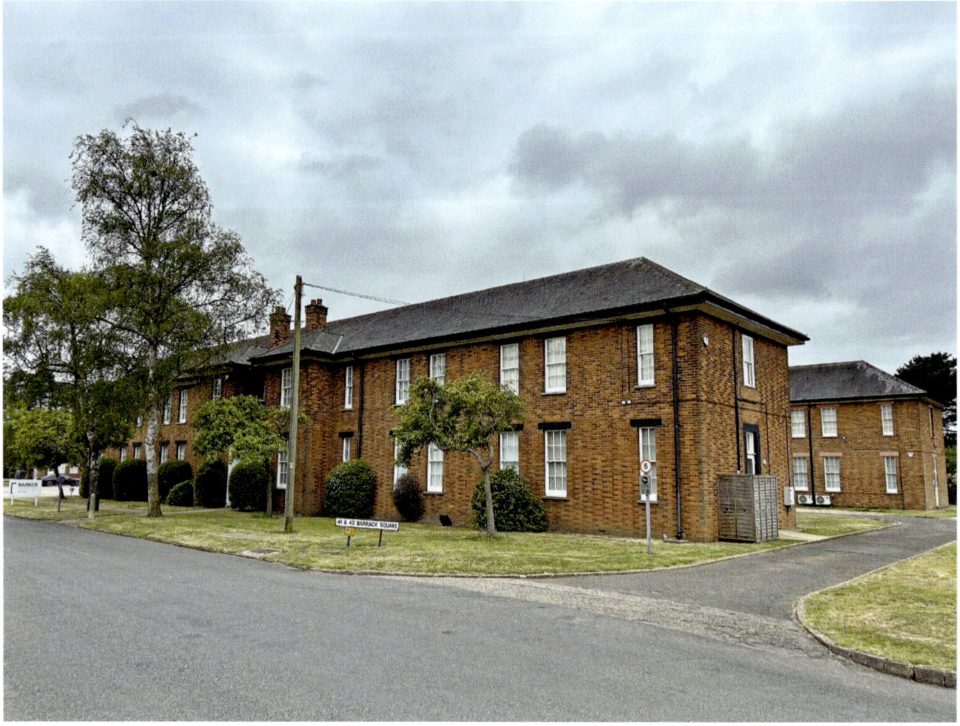

USAAF Barracks at Martlesham Heath.

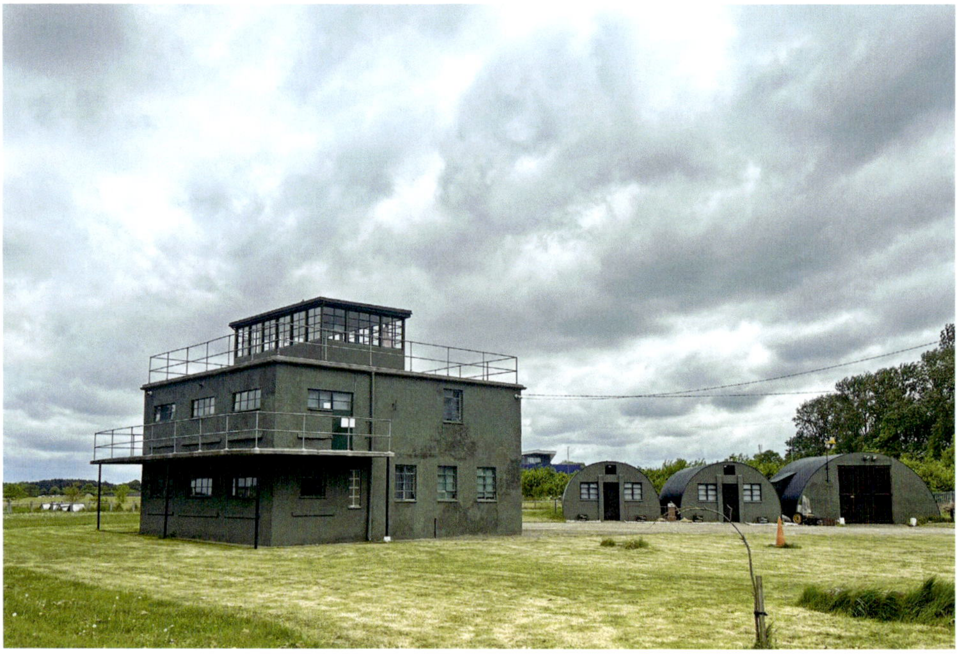

Control tower and Nissen huts at Rougham Airfield, former USAAF Station 468.

The RAF and USAAF also required facilities beyond the use of airfields, such as Advance Ammunition Parks and hospitals. Often 'ammo dumps' would use a natural cave system or dense woodland to aid their concealment; however this would be supplemented when required with concrete structures to protect the ordnance. Such sites included Warren Wood and Little Heath, which were satellite sites to RAF Barnham (which was used as a Forward Filling Depot for poisonous gas during the Second World War). North of Sudbury, near the village of Acton, the Acton Place Manor and its grounds became home to the 136th Station Hospital, and at Redgrave Park, a 200-acre country estate with a historic manor house became the 65th General Hospital. The 65th treated more than 17,000 patients between February 1944 and August 1945, providing first line treatment for the constant stream of casualties from heavy bomber crews of the 8th USAAF flying from Suffolk and all over East Anglia.

The physical reminders of the RAF and USAAF's involvement during the Second World War in Suffolk include control towers, memorials and sections of runway or perimeter track. However, the physical heritage associated with those who served isn't always bound to airfields. In the small market town of Lavenham, a standard USAAF bomber airfield was built during 1943 and was opened in April 1944; the 487th BG were based here until the end of the war. Those working the airfield, along with soldiers and airmen

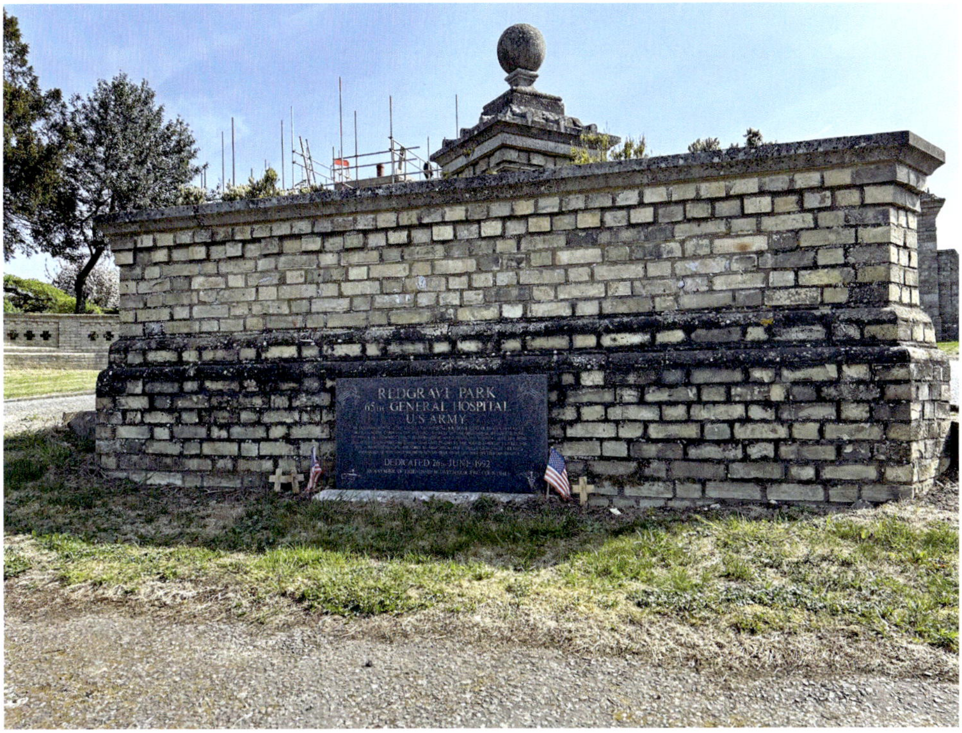

65th General Hospital memorial and gate house, Redgrave Park. Comprised of staff with connections to Duke University in North Carolina, they spent fifteen months training in military procedures at Fort Bragg, before embarking for England in 1943.

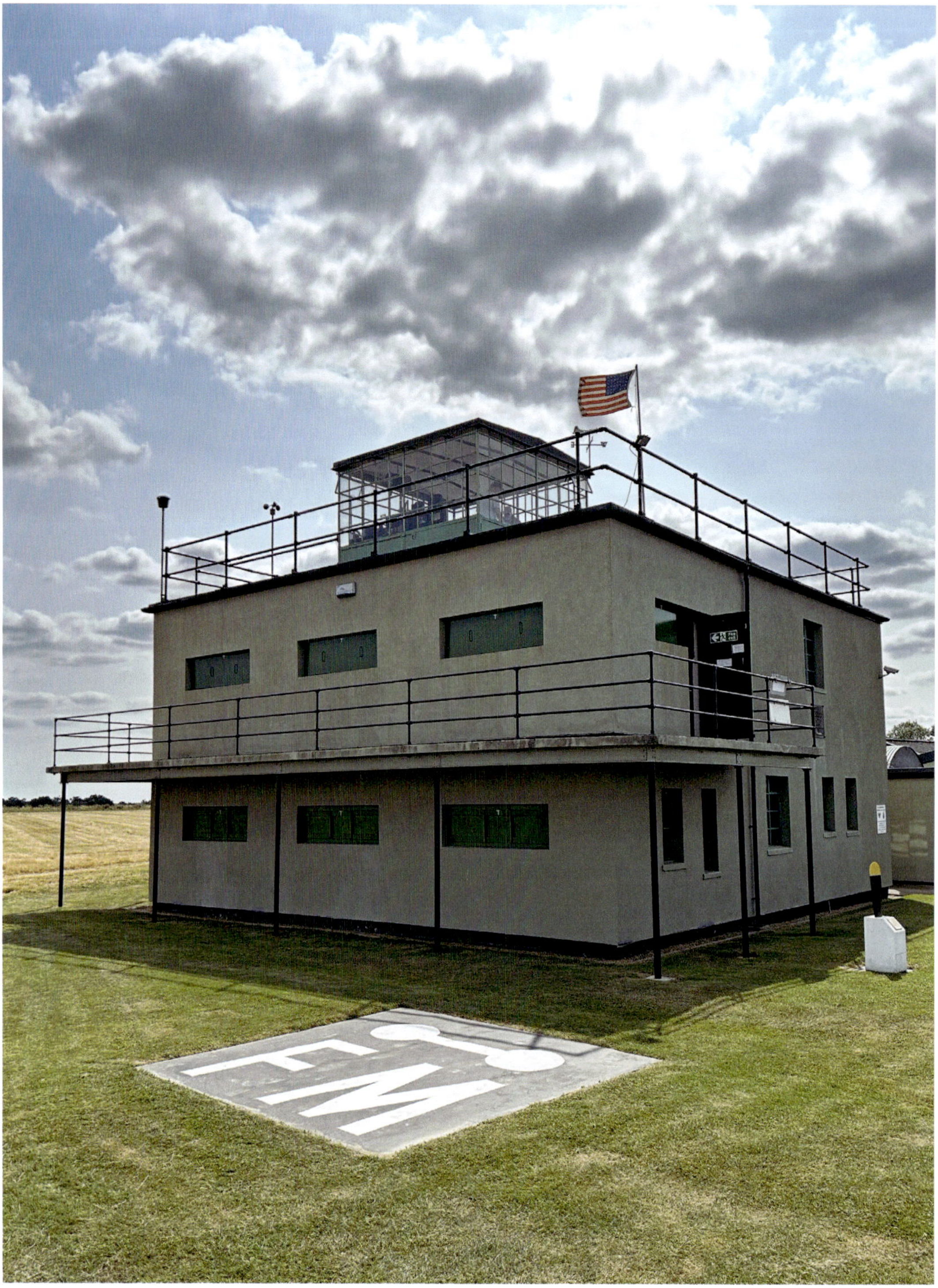

Control tower at the Parnham Airfield Museum (former USAAF Station 153) which also houses the Museum of the British Resistance Organisation and the history of the Auxiliary Units.

from neighbouring areas, frequently visited Lavenham during their downtime, with evidence of their visits in the local pub – The Swan. Those who visited throughout the war left mementos, such as formation badges, with some partaking in the 'boot challenge' – drinking three and half pints of ale from a boot-shaped glass. The record was held by Mick Wilson, who drank the boot of ale in an impressive twenty-two seconds in 1940.

As the allied forces recruited, trained and resupplied for the eventual Normandy invasion in 1944, specific preparations for the D-Day landings were well underway in Suffolk, including Operation 'Kruschen'. The aim of 'Kruschen' was to see how German defence along the Atlantic Wall could be breached, so concrete defences were built around the Dunwich Heath and Westleton Walks to simulate German defences. The ruined structures of mock anti-tank emplacements, shallow impressions of German trenches, and concrete pillboxes can still be seen today. In May 1944, at Waldringfield and Woolverston Hall, a 'dummy fleet' was constructed and moored along the rivers Stour, Orwell and Debden as part of Operation Fortitude South. The aim was to deceive the enemy into believing an invasion fleet would target the Calais area, while the true fleet amassed along the south coast. Deception had been part of British military strategy before planning the D-Day landings. In November 1940 decoy towns and cities were created with the hope to trick the enemy to drop their bombs on countryside location, using controlled fires that offered the illusion that the area had been targeted by bombs. These decoy sites were designated 'SF' sites, also known as a 'Starfish' decoy, and were sometimes combined with Civilian 'QF' sites, which replicated the dimmed light that could be seen by enemy aircraft flying overhead. Shottisham was a site that contained both 'Starfish' and Civilian 'QF' decoys, to protect the aircraft and armament production taking place at factories such as Ransome, Sims and Jefferies in Ipswich.

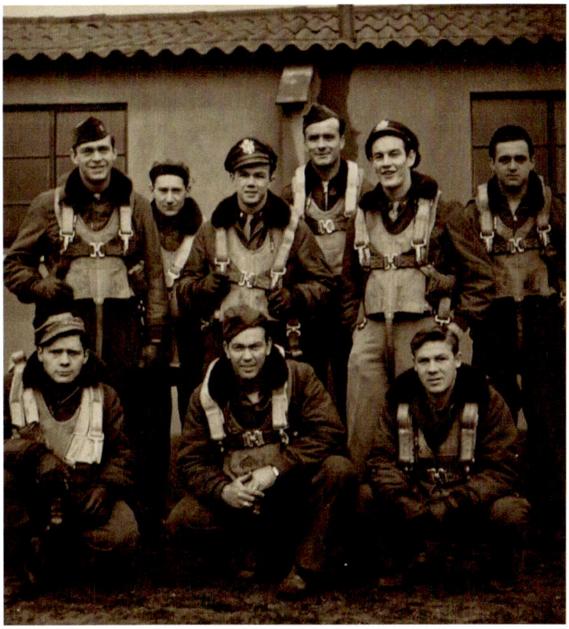

Lieutenant James H. Saunders (third from the left) and his crew at Lavenham, 16 March 1915. (National Archives D.C.)

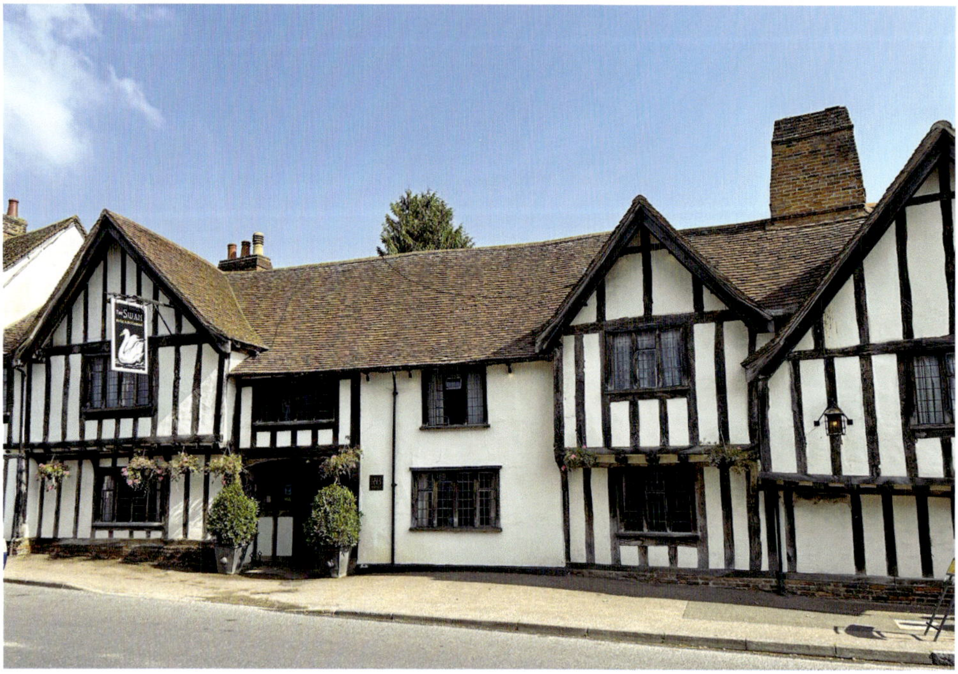

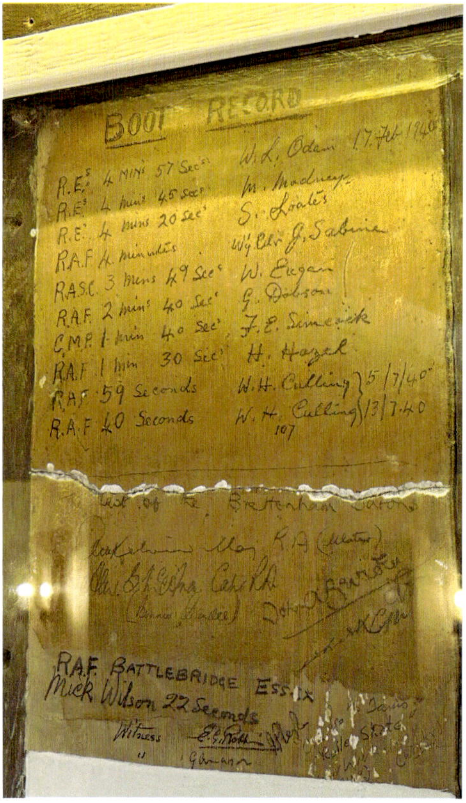

Above: The Swan Pub, Lavenham, where many US and British service personnel left their names and units on the wall of what is now the 'Airmen's Bar'.

Left: Names of those who tried the 'Boot Challenge'. Honourable mention must go to the author's namesake, 'W. H. Culling', who completed the challenge in forty seconds in July 1940, beating his earlier attempt by nineteen seconds.

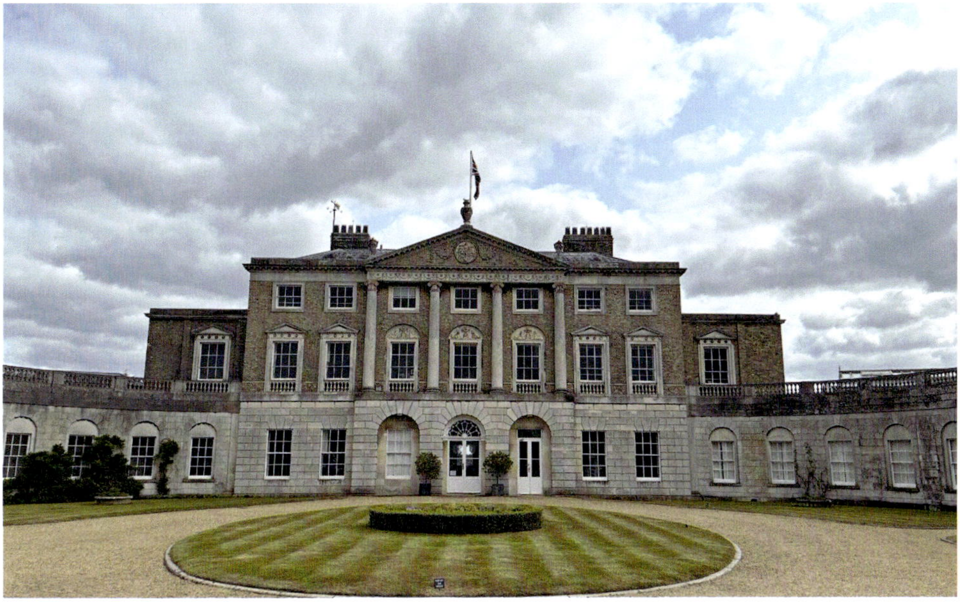

Woolverston Hall was requisitioned by the War Office in late 1939 and by the Admiralty in October 1942 for use as a Combined Operations Base and naval training establishment. It also contributed to making dummy landing craft as part of the D-Day deceptions.

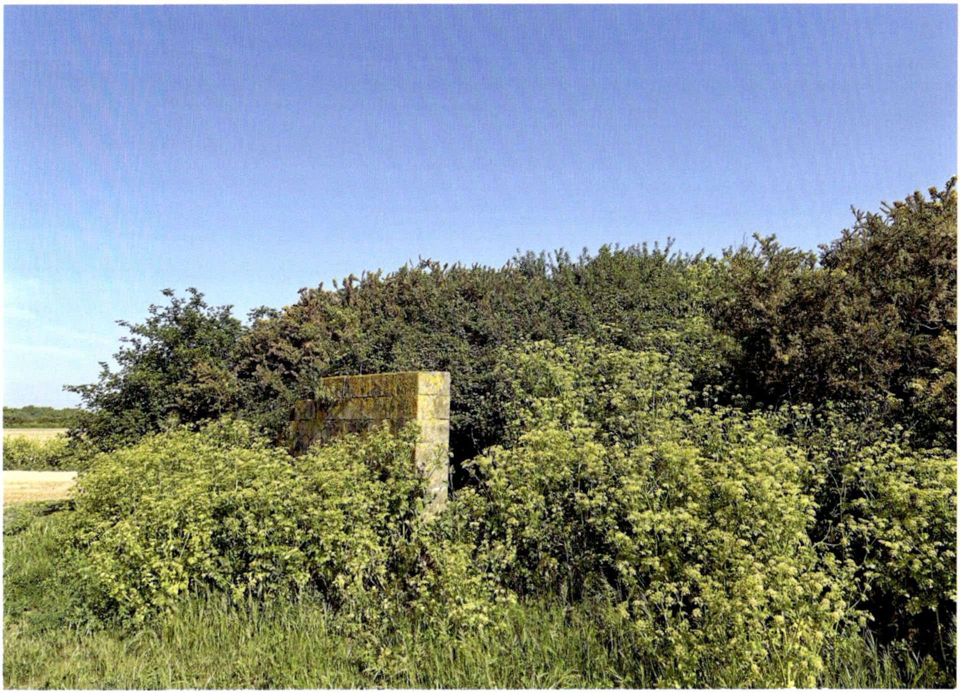

The entrance to the Shottisham 'Starfish' decoy sites operations shelter – partially submerged within an earth mound and significantly overgrown.

Post-Second World War to Present Day

By late 1945, many of the wartime airfields were slowly being returned to agriculture, and while some of the requisitioned homes were returned to their owners and restored to their former glory, others would be demolished as a result of mistreatment by the military units that occupied them, or due to a change in the owner's financial situation. The military landscape in Suffolk post-1945 is one of decline in terms of a general military footprint, but in military importance. The 'Cold War' with Soviet Union and the development of the atomic bomb are two of the most dominant features of Suffolk's post-war military heritage. At Orford Ness during the 1950s, the King's Marsh became a test range for experiments that recorded the flight paths of air-launched rockets, while in 1968 a secret radar project (code-named 'Cobra Mist') began with the aim of detecting and tracking aircraft. During this same period, buildings to carry out environmental tests on the atomic bomb were built at Orford Ness. These tests simulated the strains an atomic weapon could experience before hitting its target, such as vibrations, variations in extreme temperatures, and 'G' forces. Although no nuclear material was used at the test site, the high-explosive components the weapon were; in the event of an explosion, the test laboratories had been able to cope with the consequences. Nuclear material for Britain's weapons was stored elsewhere in Suffolk, separate from the environmental test areas. In the early 1950s, RAF Barnham became a dedicated storage and maintenance facility for Britain's first nuclear weapon – 'Blue Danube'. This storage facility was

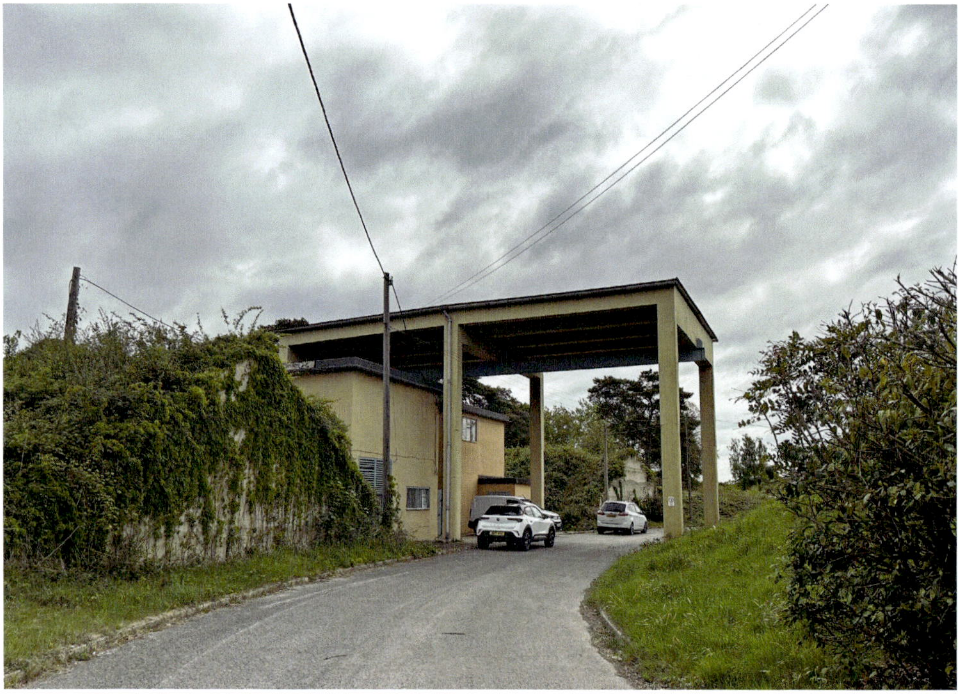

The former RAF Barnwell site for storing Britain's Blue Danube nuclear bombs. This building, with a large lifting gantry, was used to house the large non-nuclear component of the bomb.

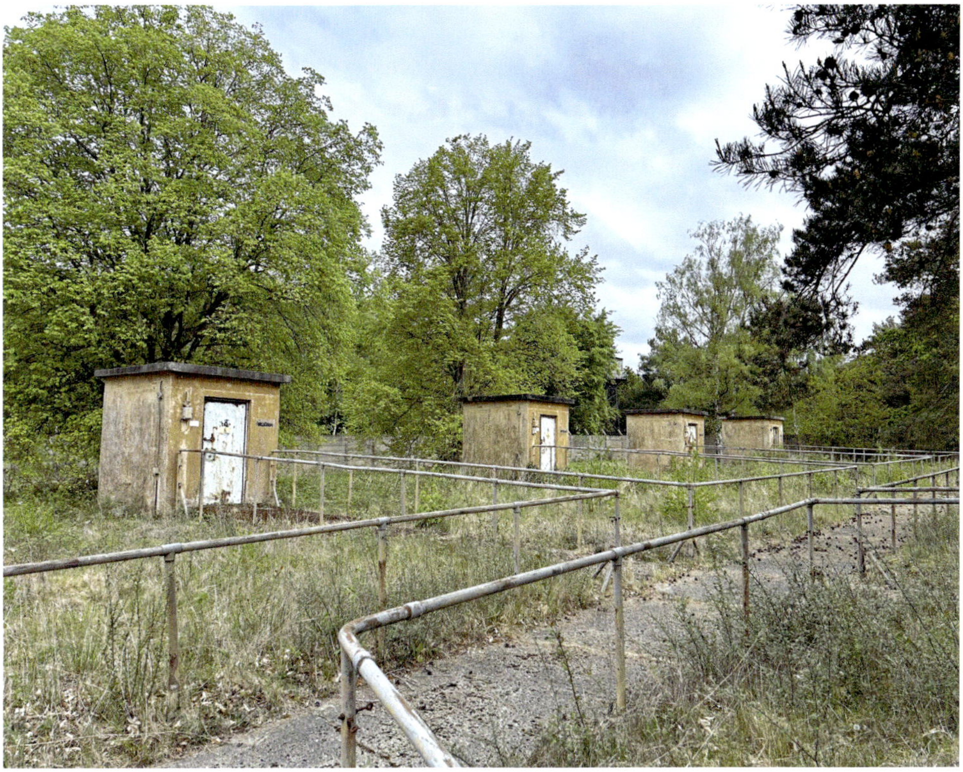

These 'hutches' were used to store each Blue Danube's fissile core. A 'trefoil' – the symbol warning of ionizing radiation – can still be seen on some of the doors.

short-lived, however, as the 10,000-lb and 24-feet-long free-fall bomb was soon obsolete; the development of air-launched rocket-propelled missiles led to Britain adopting the 'Blue Steel' nuclear weapon for its V-bomber fleet in late 1962. The nuclear storage section of RAF Barham closed in the early 1960s and is now part of the Gorse Industrial Estate.

Not all the land used to build Suffolk's many Second World War airfields were returned to their former owners. Construction work to build RAF Bentwaters began in late 1942, to accommodate the thousands of USAAF forces that were arriving in East Anglia. Due to various complications, the airfield remained unfinished and, by mid-1944, the USAAF no longer required additional airfields, and transferred RAF Bentwaters back to the Air Ministry. The RAF discontinued flying operations at RAF Bentwaters in July 1950, and the airfield was placed under care and maintenance until it was once again transferred to the US Air Force. Numerous US Fighter Squadrons were stationed at Bentwaters throughout the Cold War, with the Americans leaving the base in 1993. Many of the original features not only survive but are accessible to the public. Built during the base's modernisation in the 1970s, the hardened command-post is now home to the Bentwaters Cold War Museum, which features the original decontamination showers and air-lock, and a War Operations Room. Suffolk was also home to other Cold War defences such as

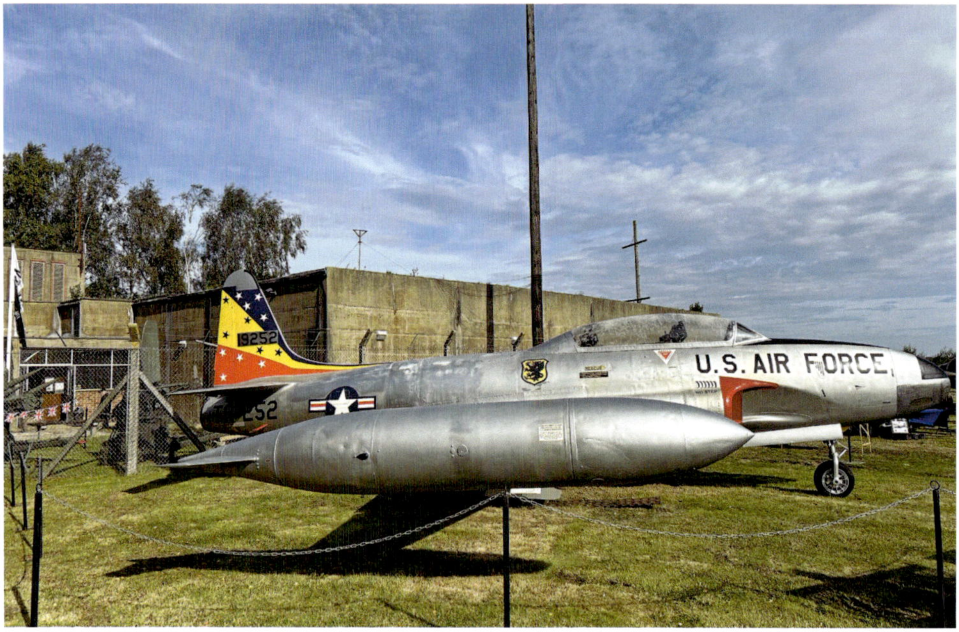

A Lockheed T-33A aircraft outside the Bentwaters Cold War Museum. The museum building is the former USAF Command Post.

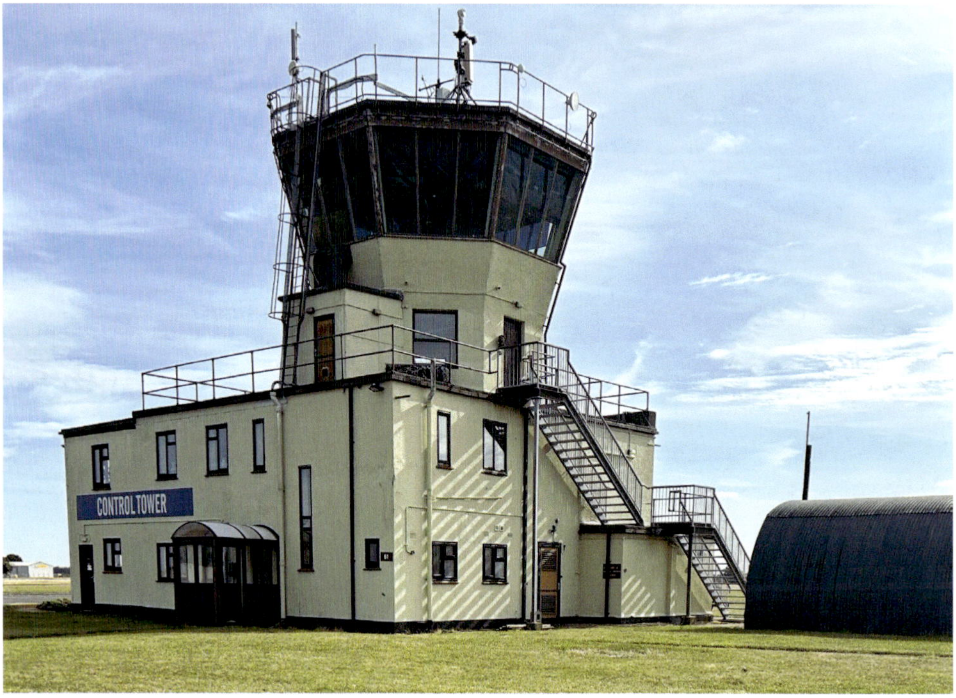

Originally built during the Second World War, the control tower at RAF Bentwaters was adapted and used by the USAF during the Cold War.

the 'Bloodhound' surface-to-air missile. This was positioned in three areas of Suffolk – Rattlesden, Wattisham and Bawdsey – until the missile's decommission in 1991.

The years that followed the Second World War and Cold War era marked a continued decline in Suffolk's military presence. As the British Army and RAF became much smaller after the Second World War, so did their presence in Suffolk's towns and villages. Despite this, the military remains part of the identity of many Suffolk's communities. After several amalgamations, the Royal Anglian Regiment, successors to the Suffolk Regiment, still have Company detachments in Lowestoft and Bury St Edmunds, with the Regimental Headquarters located at the old Suffolk Regiment Depot, Gibraltar Barracks in Bury St Edmunds. The British Army also has other regiments stationed at various locations throughout Suffolk, including at the former Second World War airfield at Woodbridge, which today includes Rock Barracks (home of 23 Parachute Engineer Regiment, Royal Engineers) and Woodbridge Airfield, used by the Army Air Corps for training exercises.

While many of Suffolk's military airfields built prior to and during the Second World War no longer exist, four still play a prominent role in maintaining global security. Two of these are RAF Honington and RAF Wattisham. Built in 1937, RAF Honington would be home to RAF and Czechoslovakian Bomber Squadron, until handed over to the USAAF in 1942 where it served as a repair depot for B-17 bombers and later a base for the 364th Fighter Group. The airfield was returned to the RAF in 1946 and remains an active RAF establishment to this day as the Headquarters for the RAF Regiment and RAF Police,

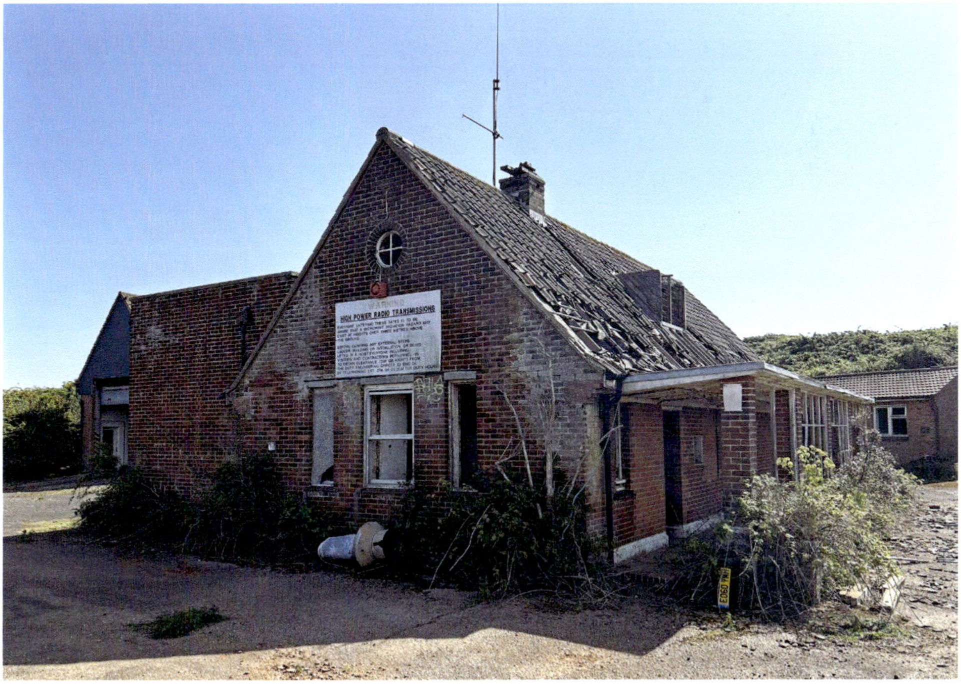

The former entrance to RAF Bawdsey's Bloodhound missile site.

as well as 28 Regiment, Royal Engineers, who provide the Defence Counter-Chemical Biological Radiological and Nuclear capability. Similarly, built in 1939, RAF Wattisham was used initially as a RAF bomber station, was transferred to the USAAF in 1942 and hosted US fighter units before being returned to the RAF in 1946. The RAF left in 1992 once the Cold War threat had passed and they transferred the station to the British Army the following year. The site is now known as the Wattisham Flying Station and is home to Apache helicopter force of 3 and 4 Regiment, Army Air Corps.

While it may not compare to the scale of the 'Friendly Invasion' between 1942 and 1945, there is still a strong US military presence in the county, as they occupy the former RAF Bomber Command airfields at Mildenhall and Lakenheath. Serving as RAF Bomber base for the entire Second World War, the USAF arrived in 1948 and remain there today. Over its eighty-plus-year history, RAF Lakenheath and the residents of the surrounding villages have witnessed various aircraft being flown from the base, such as the Second World War Wellington and Stirling bombers, to the post-war American Boeing B-29 Superfortress and B-47 Stratojet and, in more recent years, the Lockheed Martin F-35A Lightning II stealth fighter.

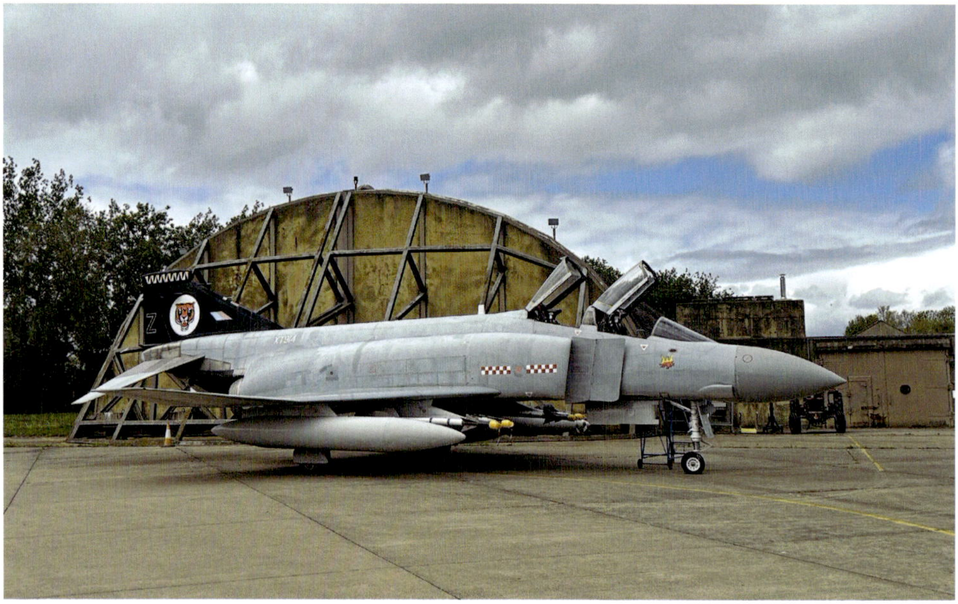

A McDonnell Douglass Phantom FRG2 aircraft outside a Hardened Aircraft Shelter (HAS). The HAS was built to withstand a direct hit from a 1,000-lb bomb.

The Gears of War

Suffolk's military contribution extends beyond the county's men and women who served in the armed forces and the defensive structures that dot the coastal and rural landscape. While the Industrial Revolution provided the technology to produce wartime munitions on an unprecedented scale, for centuries prior, Suffolk's workers contributed to the nation's ability to wage war. In the seventeenth century, shipbuilding became major industry in Woodbridge, in part due to the abundance of quality timber in the area. So much so that Phineas Pett, a Master Shipwright from Deptford, concluded that it would be far easier to build men-of-war ships for the Royal Navy in Woodbridge than transport the timber to other dockyards. At least fifteen men-of-war were built and rigged with rope made in Woodbridge between 1630 and 1680, after which commercial vessels continued to be built there; the *Maidstone* – a forty-gun, fourth-rate frigate – was built in Woodbridge for the Commonwealth Navy in 1654. Following the Restoration of the Monarchy in 1660,

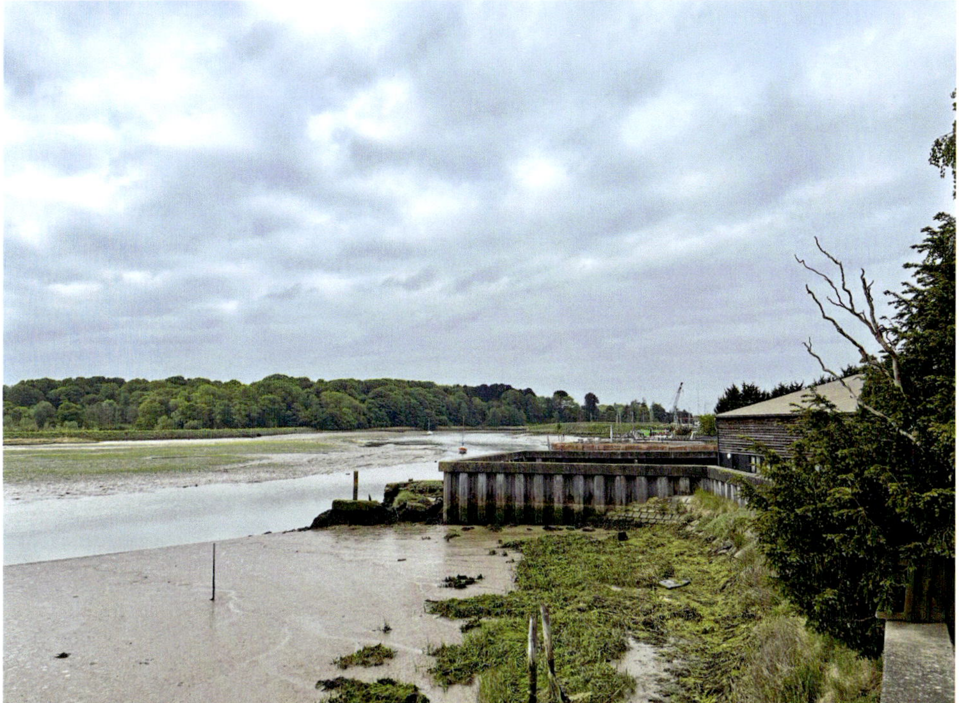

View of the River Debden at Woodridge with Lime Kiln Quay on the right-hand side. This is where Phineas Pett's son, Peter, built the first Royal Navy ships at Woodbridge.

the vessel was renamed HMS *Mary Rose*. She saw service during the Anglo-Dutch Wars and defeated a force of seven Algerian ships during the Battle of Cádiz in 1669.

The seventeenth century saw the transition from the use of pikemen and musketeers by English armies to predominantly using musketeers. The pike was abandoned altogether by the British in 1705. In 1722 the British Army introduced a muzzle-loading flintlock 'Land Pattern Musket', more commonly known as the 'Brown Bess', and with it began a new industry of not only producing the muskets, but also all-important flint. By the late eighteenth century there were several businesses producing flint in places like Maidstone and Purfleet, however the small market town of Brandon produced such high-quality black flint (good for fifty shots) that Brandon flint masters became the sole suppliers to the Board of Ordnance during the Napoleonic Wars. They supplied over 1,000,000 musket flints per month to the Board of Ordnance in 1813. After the Battle of Waterloo, the British Army was reduced in size and the large contracts for Brandon to produce black flints to the army ceased. Despite this, millions of Brandon flints continued to be made and shipped around the world, continuing into the twentieth century.

Flint was not the only ordnance-related product supplied by Suffolk industry. In 1861, Messrs Prentice established the Great Eastern Chemical Works in Stowmarket, and in early 1864 began to produce guncotton – a replacement for gunpowder to be used in military and commercial explosives. The works would be renamed numerous times over the next century and a half, including the Patent Safety Guncotton Company Limited in 1870. The company received a government licence to produce explosives using a new method, patented by the War Office chemist Frederick Abel. His new method introduced the process of pulping and pressing, allowing cheaper cotton waste to be used in place of expensive materials. Unfortunately, the Patent Safety Guncotton Company did not live up to its name and in August 1871, a huge explosive almost destroyed the factory and extensively damaged nearby properties, leaving a crater 10 feet deep and 40 feet wide, and killed twenty-three people. Despite this devastating accident, a new factory was under construction by the end of the year. The company was renamed several times after the accident, before finally settling with the New Explosives Company Limited in 1885. At the outbreak of war in 1914, the government relied on the Royal Gunpowder Factory at Waltham Abbey for their military explosives, however the increased demand required assistance from private firms such as the New Explosives Factory, who were already contractors to the Admiralty by 1913. During the war the site produced guncotton alongside cordite, a smokeless explosive that was used in single-part cased military ammunition. Over 2,000 workers were employed on day and night shifts, many of whom were female. After the First World War, the demand for explosives from commercial companies ceased, and the factory focused on manufacturing cellulose lacquers under the name Necol Industrial Collodions Limited.

Suffolk's early contribution to government munitions wasn't completely centred around the production of ordnance. In the eighteenth century, Sudbury weavers produced a lightweight woven textile called 'bunting' for the Royal Navy. Bunting was not only used by the British military but also exported for use by the United States military – surprisingly during a time when the two nations were at war. During the war of 1812, Fort McHenry protected Baltimore from British attacks from Chesapeake Bay. In 1814,

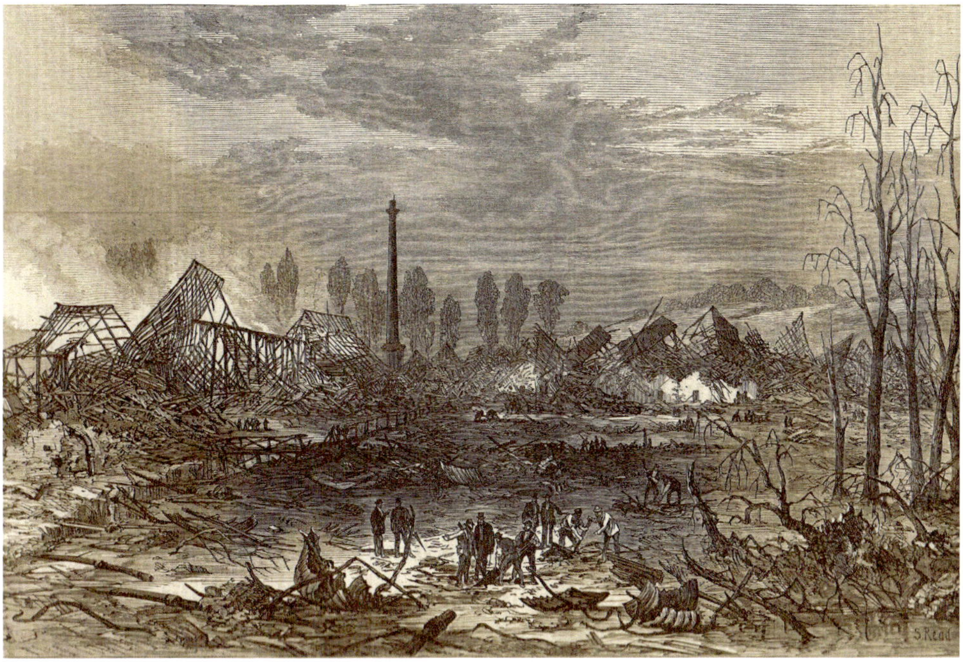

Print showing the aftermath of the Stowmarket guncotton explosion.

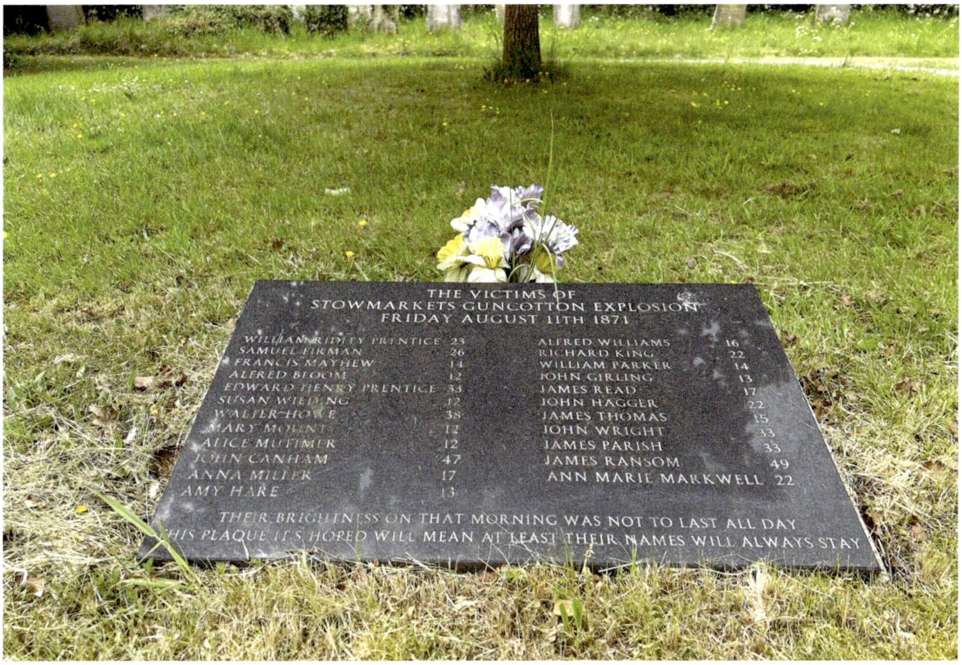

Stowmarket explosion memorial at Stowmarket's Old Cemetery. The explosion killed more than twenty-three workers, including two of the Prentice family. Another seventy were injured and there were 180 cases of deafness caused by the intense sound pressure from the blast.

the fort required a 30 by 42-foot 'Stars and Stripes' garrison flag and they commissioned local flag-maker Mary Pickersgill to make one. A large amount of bunting was required, and – despite war with Britain – merchant ships carried bunting made in Sudbury to be used in this flag. Following the decisive victory at the Battle of Bladensburg and the subsequent burning of the White House and Capitol a few weeks earlier, the British attacked the fort on 13 September 1814. Despite the Royal Navy's best efforts, it failed to capture the fort, sparing Baltimore from the same fate as Washington, DC. In the morning of 14 September 1814, the garrison flag flew from Fort McHenry, signifying America's resilience against the British attack, and would go on to be the inspiration for US national anthem 'The Star-Spangled Banner'. Many towns in Suffolk have centuries-long links to the textile industry. For example, D. Gurteens & Sons of Haverhill founded the Chauntry Mills in 1784 and specialised in weaving 'Drabbets', a material used for making agricultural smocks. Gurteens received its first government contract in 1905, producing khaki clothing, and at the outbreak of war in 1914 the business was fully occupied with the production of services' clothing. The company's version of the 1902 pattern tunic used by British forces was officially approved on 7 December 1914.

In May 1915, representatives of manufacturing from Suffolk, Norfolk and Essex met at the Great Eastern Hotel in Liverpool Street, London, to discuss whether the area's munitions contributions would be better met by creating either a national factory or by forming a cooperative. The latter was chosen, and in doing so the East Anglian Munitions Committee was formed. Seventeen firms from Suffolk worked for the committee and, despite East Anglia not being known as a manufacturing district, out of a total of forty-two munition-producing districts, East Anglia's output was third only behind London and Manchester. The Committee built a central depot at Ransomes and Rapier Ltd in Ipswich (which, prior to the war, produced heavy railway equipment), to handle the painting, rectifications, revarnishing, cleaning and inspections from the War Office. Employing between 300 and 400 workers, mostly women, the staff worked day and night. Women were employed in roles such as canteen workers, welfare and ambulance department, motor drivers, clerical and technical duties. By the end of the war, 2,133,000 shells passed through the Committee's depot. A contract for 4.5-inch shells was tasked to seven of the cooperatives to manufacture, which included five Suffolk firms: R. Boby & Co. Ltd of Bury St Edmunds; Garrett & Sons Ltd of Leiston; E. R. F. Turner Ltd; Ransomes and Rapier Ltd; and Ransomes, Sims and Jefferies Ltd. All of these firms were based in Ipswich. While the Committee's major contribution to the war effort was the production of shells, the individual firms each had other contracts for munitions, either as part of the cooperative or direct contracts. J. W. Brooke & Co. Ltd of Lowestoft and Reavell & Co. Ltd of Ipswich were two of the four Committee firms with contracts to make fuses for high-explosive shells, producing 4,700,000 despite brass shortages forcing the adoption of a cast-iron body (which required time to work out how to make them rust proof). Reavell & Co. also had a contract to produce air compressors for recuperators of guns, along with gyroscopic sights to drop bombs from aeroplanes.

Despite Wilfrid Stokes of Ransomes and Napier being elected as Chairman of the East Anglian Munitions Committee, his time was occupied with the development and production of his weapon and its bomb, the 'Stokes mortar'. Firing between twenty-five

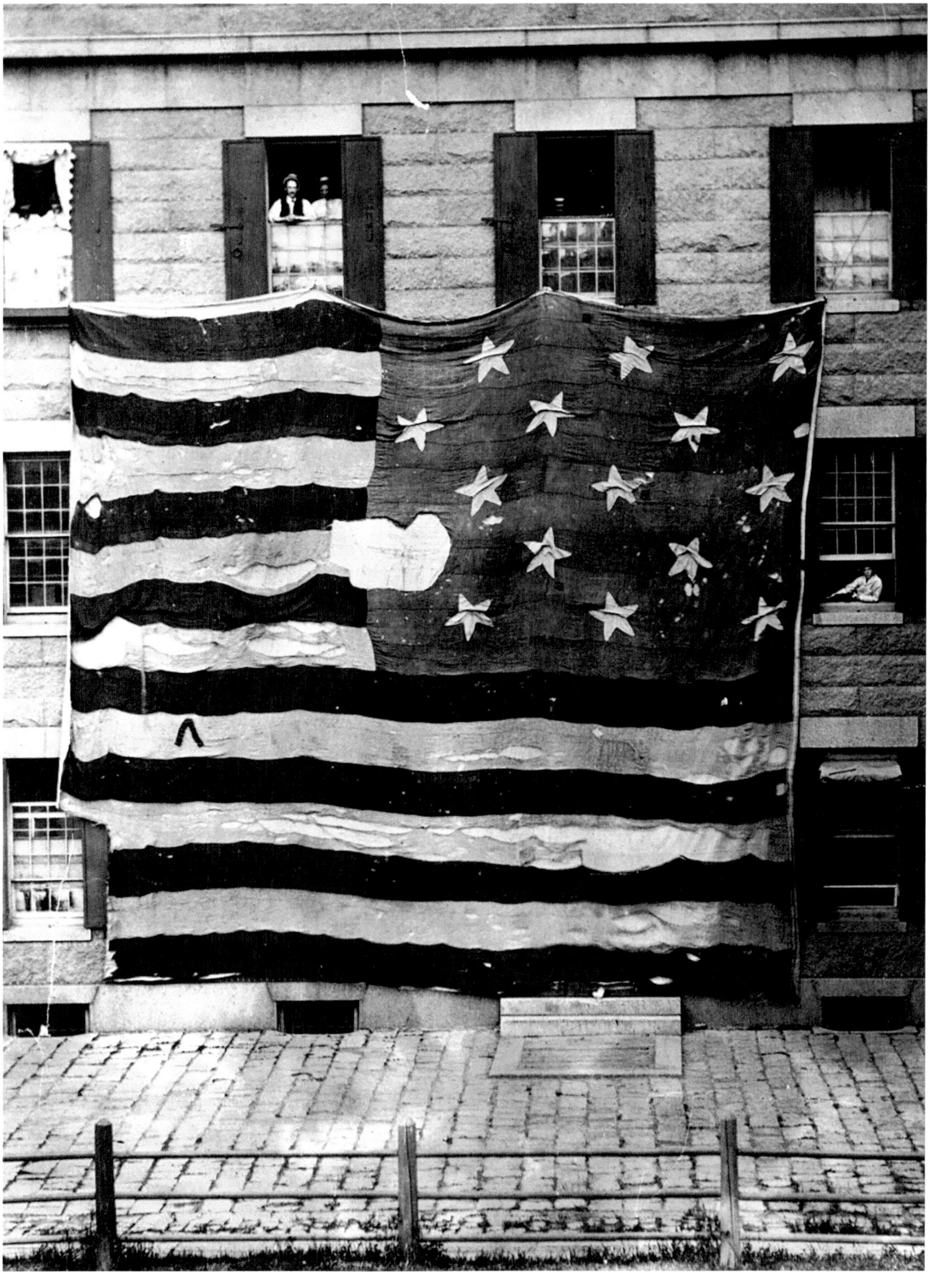

The Fort McHenry Flag, made from bunting produced in Sudbury. (Naval History and Heritage Command)

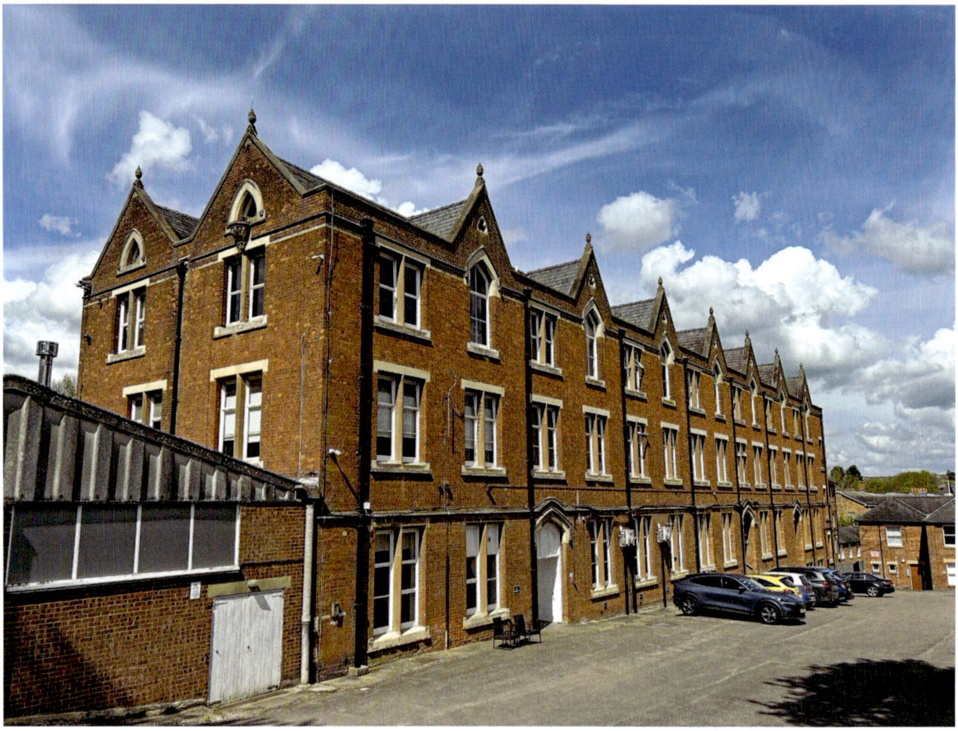

Gurteen's Chauntry Mill in Haverhill, built in 1784.

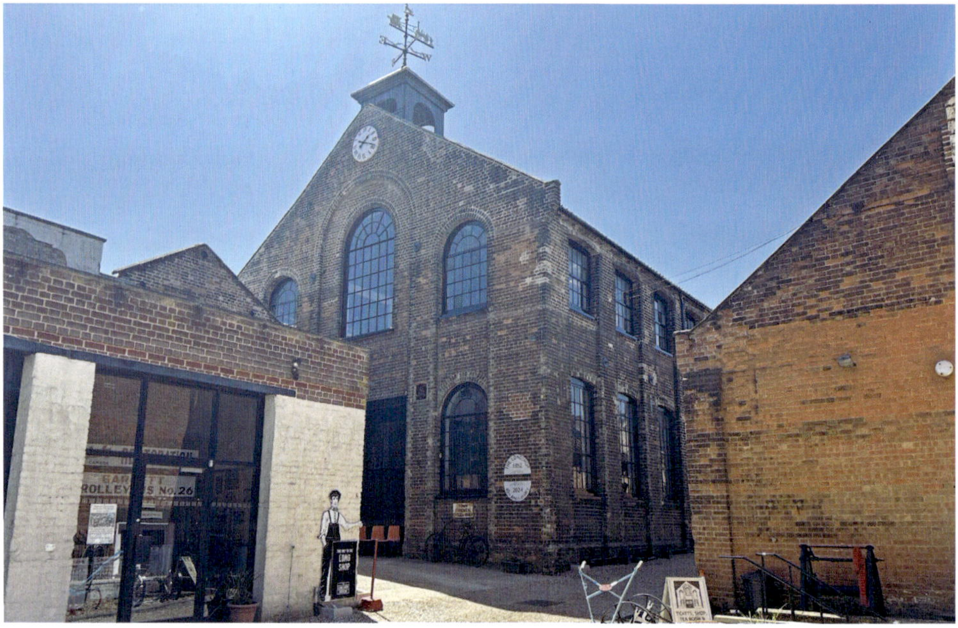

Garrett's 'Long Shop' in Leiston, opened in 1853 and operating the first production line, contributed to the county's munitions production.

and thirty rounds per minute at a range of over 750 yards, the new mortar was designed to be mobile enough to be used an infantry support weapon and had made its way to the Western Front by late 1915. Not all of Suffolk's First World War munitions were produced by the East Anglian Munitions Committee. F. Tibbenham's furniture-making business in Ipswich made aeroplane propellers, while the Maconochie Brothers' factory constructed their 'No. 1 Factory' in Lowestoft in 1915–16, where they continued to produce soldiers' rations, having first secured a contract to do so during the Second Boer War. Their most infamous creation was the Maconochie's Stew, often referred to as 'meat and vegetable rations'. This could be eaten hot or cold, however the former was difficult for those in the trenches, and the latter was considered unpalatable.

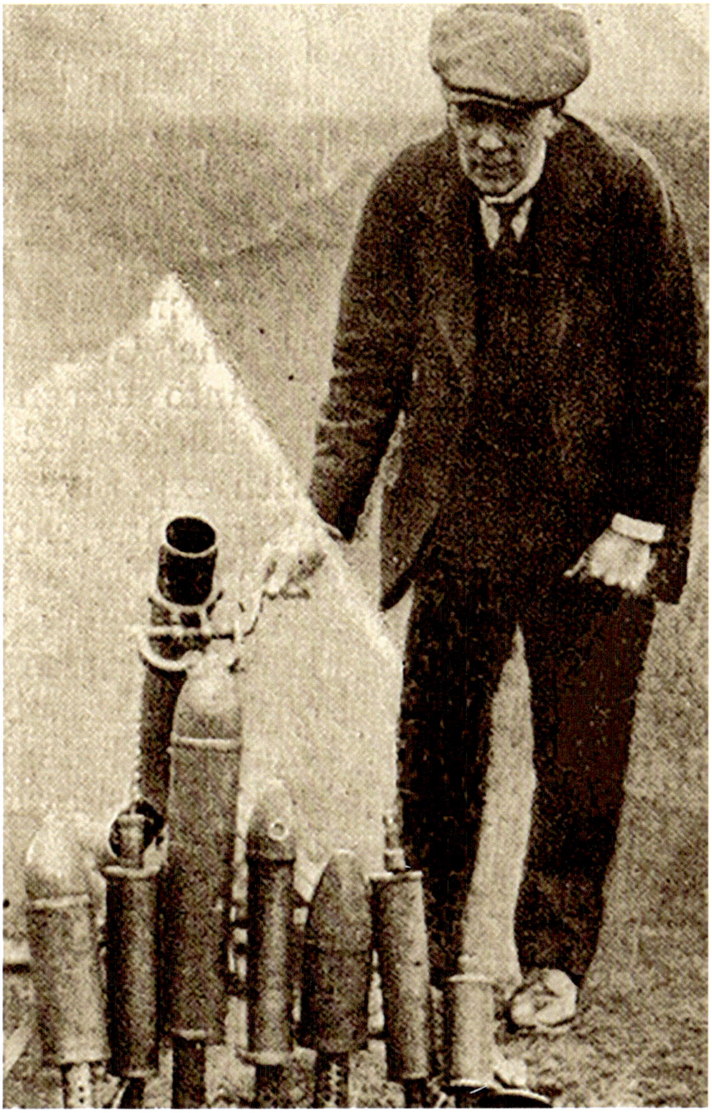

Wilfred Stokes with his invention – the 'Stokes mortar'. For his work, Stokes was made a Knight Commander of the Most Excellent Order of the British Empire (KBE) in 1917.

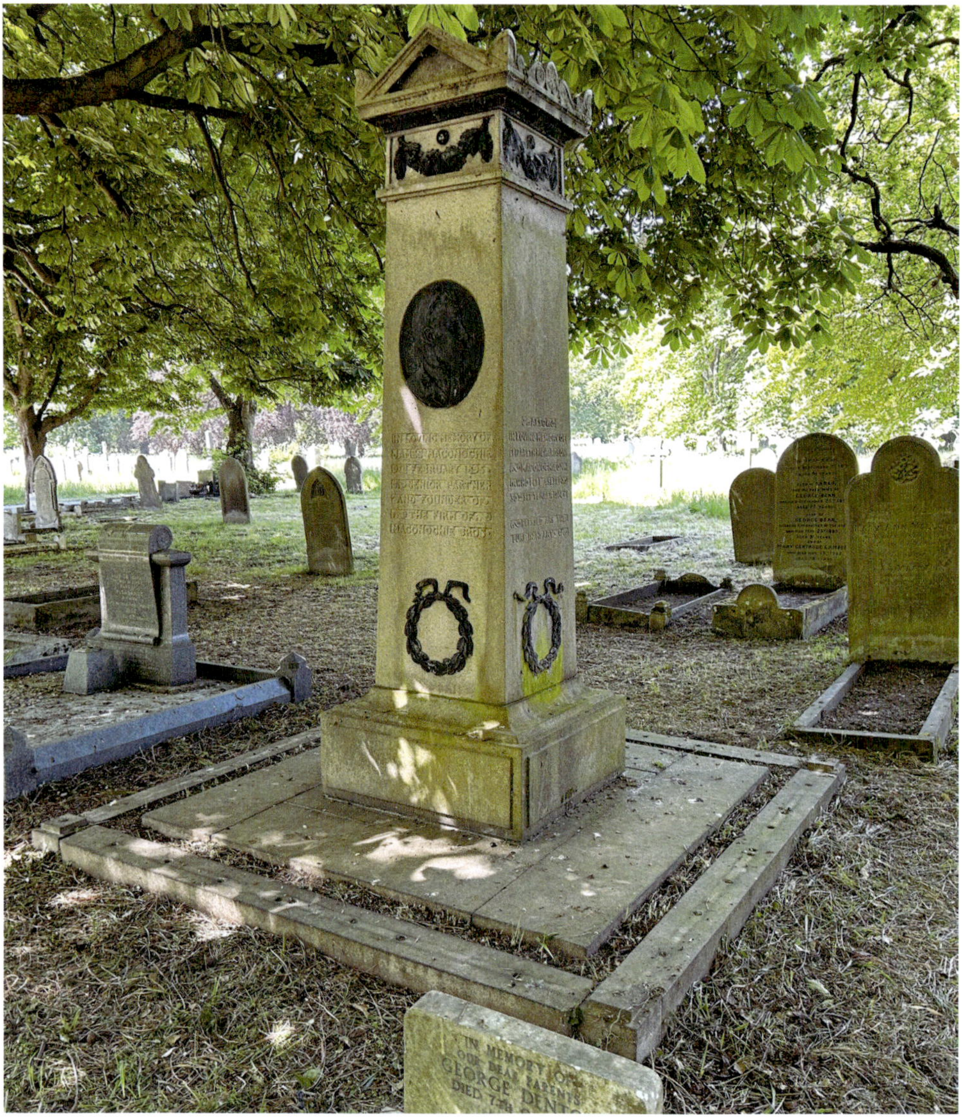

Memorial to James Maconochie who, along with his brother Archibald, started the Maconochie Brothers business in Lowestoft in 1873.

The Second World War once again required the assistance from Suffolk's manufacturing firms, many of whom had War Office contracts during the First World War. The Gurteens factory in Haverhill continued to produce military clothing during the Second World War, while Tibbenham's in Ipswich crafted the wooden components of the Bren gun. S. Richards & Co. Ltd of Lowestoft, whose premises had been used producing munitions during the First World War, had reverted back to shipbuilding after the war and continued to build vessels for the Admiralty during the Second World War, including minesweepers, torpedo recovery vessels, and Victualling Inshore Crafts. Shipbuilders based at Oulton Boad, near Lowestoft, had to adjust their pre-war building of pleasure crafts for hire to accepting wartime contracts from the Admiralty. Collins Pleasecrafts Co. Ltd, Leo Robinson, and Brooke Marine (known as J. W. Brooke & Co.) all built the Fairmile B Class Motor Launch (ML). Arriving in kit form, these shipbuilders assembled dozens of these vessels which had been designed for coastal protection from submarine threats. A majority of ML were built for the Royal Navy, however some were sent to other navies, including the Free French and Hellenic navies. One of the ships, ML 262, assembled by Collins and commissioned in June 1941, formed part of the Royal Navy force that took part on the ill-fated St Nazaire Raid on the coast of Brittany. The objective of the Commando force being carried in the ML was to destroy the German dry-dock, forcing the German battleships to return to home waters for repair. Unfortunately – like many of the MLs involved in the attack – ML 262 was destroyed, with its crew either killed or taken prisoner.

At the end of the Second World War the demand for munitions on a large scale ceased, and while many of the firms went back to making their pre-war products, developing and expanding their product range, others would merge or simply stopped trading. Despite this, military manufacturing did continue in Suffolk, albeit on a substantially smaller scale. Brooke Marine, who contributed its resources to both world wars, would continue to use its technical expertise in shipbuilding to build vessels for the US Navy, Royal Australian Navy, and Royal Navy of Oman. Three Edenton Class salvage and rescue ships were built for the US Navy: USS *Edenton* (ATS-1), USS *Beaufort* (ATS-2), and USS *Brunswick* (ATS-3). The ships were commissioned into service between 1970 and 1972; all three were decommissioned in 1996 with two of them having served in the Pacific and based at Pearl Harbor. The Brooke Marine shipbuilding site now lies dormant, awaiting residential redevelopment.

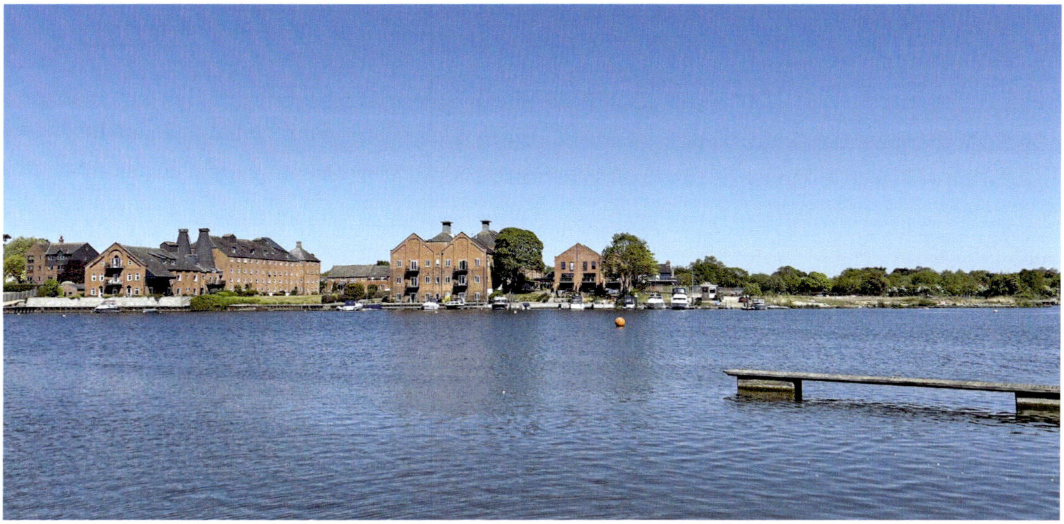

View of the Oulton Broads from Nicholas Everitt Park. Collins Pleasurecrafts would have operated from the cleared site to the right.

Gallant and Distinguished Suffolk

There are many men and women from Suffolk who distinguished themselves during war, from their brave conduct or years of invaluable service to the nation's military. Some are Suffolk born and bred, others find their way to the county later in life, and for many Suffolk is a temporary home away from home. There are several who have been officially recognised by their government and monarchy through medals for gallantry or orders of chivalry; there are also many others who receive nothing more than admiration for their conduct and far more that go unreported or unrecognised.

The Victoria Cross (VC), the highest award for gallantry in Britain, was instituted by Royal Warrant on 29 January 1856 to recognise extreme acts of bravery in the presence of the enemy by many soldiers and sailors who served during the Crimean War. It was during the Crimean War that in 1855 Suffolk-born Alfred Ablett received the first of many VCs earned by those associated with the county. Sergeant Ablett, born in Weybread on the Suffolk-Norfolk border near Harleston, served in the 3rd Battalion, Grenadier Guards. During the Crimean War his Battalion was present during the Siege of Sebastopol when on 2 September 1855, he witnessed a live shell land with its fuse still burning. With ammunition and powder a short distance away, with complete disregard to his own safety he immediately seized the shell and threw it out of the trench, saving is comrades from a potentially devastating explosion. Ablett was one of many who attended the first investiture of the VC at Hyde Park on 26 June 1857, having his medal pinned to his uniform by Queen Victoria. Sadly, Ablett's personal life was plagued by tragedy, with the death of his first wife and another being committed to an asylum, and the loss of several of his children at a painfully young age. Having been invalided out of the army in 1862, Ablett managed to gain a position as a Drill Sergeant with 'A' Company, 4th (Harleston) Battalion Norfolk Rifle Volunteers. During a night of excessive drinking in 1868, Ablett – possibly struggling with the tragic events in his life – attempted to 'blow his brains out' and 'was sorry he had not succeeded', as was reported in the *Norwich News* during the subsequent court proceedings. Thankfully, Ablett was found not guilty of his attempted suicide and would later find long-term employment as an inspector for the London Docks Police. Following his death in Poplar, London, in 1897, Ablett was buried in St Andrew's churchyard of his home village of Weybread, attended by representatives of the Grenadier Guards and the Harleston Rifle Volunteers. The final tragedy in Ablett's life, or more appropriately his death, is that his grave is now lost to time.

There are many more recipients of the VC from Suffolk whose gallant deeds are worthy of being explored in greater detail than this chapter allows, such as Henry Addison from Bardwell, who served with the 43rd (Monmouth) Light Infantry during the Indian Mutiny in 1859. He defended a wounded officer from rebel attacks and was in turn himself severely wounded, requiring the amputation of his left leg above the knee.

Addison died in 1887 and is buried in Bardwell's Peter & St Paul churchyard. Thomas Crisp, from Lowestoft, like many others in the area, made his living from the sea as a fisherman and in the Merchant Navy. During the First World War he joined the Royal Naval Reserve (RNR). As Skipper of HM Armed Smack 'Nelson', a Special Service 'Q' Ship (an armed fishing trawler), Crisp and his crew were fishing in the North Sea on 15 August 1917 when they were attacked by a German U-boat. Despite being mortally wounded by a shell, his legs shattered and partially disembowelled, the skipper continued to direct the crew until their ammunition was exhausted and they were forced to abandon the vessel. His crew survived, but Crisp was lost at sea. Skipper Thomas Crisp was awarded the VC posthumously, with his son Thomas William Crisp accepting the award for his father's bravery from King George V at Buckingham Palace in December 1917.

Not all of Suffolk's VC recipients were native to the county. For many people from overseas who were stationed in Suffolk during wartime, Suffolk became their home away from home, and their bravery is duly remembered. Rawdon Hume Middleton, from Sydney, Australia, enlisted in the Royal Australian Air Force in October 1940, and following flight training in Australia and Canada, arrived in Britain in February 1941. In February 1942, Middleton was posted to 149 Squadron, Royal Air Force, beginning his operational career at the rank of Flight Sergeant and flying Stirling bombers from RAF Mildenhall. Pilot Officer Middleton, having been commissioned on 15 November 1942, flew his twenty-ninth operation flight to bomb the Fiat Works in Turin, Italy, on

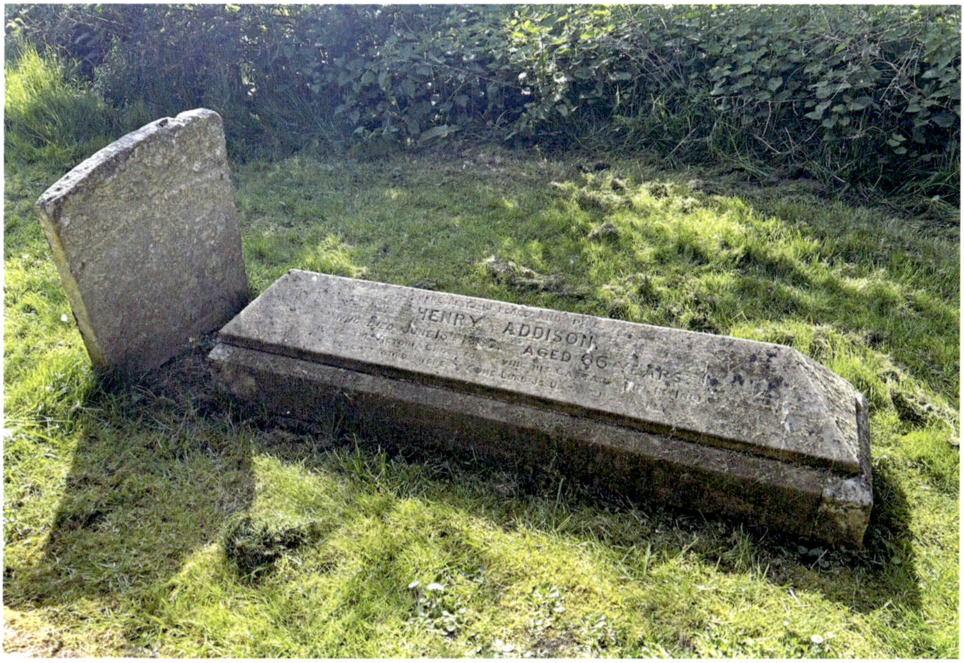

The grave of Henry Addison VC at Bardwell's Peter and St Paul churchyard. Addison received his VC at an investiture at Windsor Castle in 1860, and after being invalided out of the army, returned to Bardwell where he lived the rest of his life.

28 November. Middelton's aircraft was struck by a barrage of flak while flying over his target, damaging his aircraft and wounding Middleton in the face including injuring his right eye. Realising that the aircraft was severely damaged and lacked enough fuel to make it home, Middelton hoped that reaching the English coast would give the crew the best opportunity to bail out to safety. Upon reaching the English coast and with fuel reserves at a critical level, Middleton ordered the crew to abandon the aircraft. Pilot Officer Middleton died when his Striling bomber crashed into the sea. His body would be washed ashore at Dover on 1 February 1943. For his bravery, Middelton was awarded the VC posthumously and is buried in the churchyard of St John's in Beck Row, close to where he began his final mission.

During the 'Friendly Invasion' by the US Army Air Force to East Anglia from 1942 onwards, countless heroic acts were carried out by pilots and their crews flying from Suffolk airfields. Frederick Castle was one of the original officers selected to accompany Major General Eaker to England to form the US 8th Air Force. Between early 1942 to 1944, Castle rose through the ranks, from Captain to Brigadier General, commanding the 94th Bombardment (Bomb) Group in June 1943 and the 4th Combat Bomb Wing in April

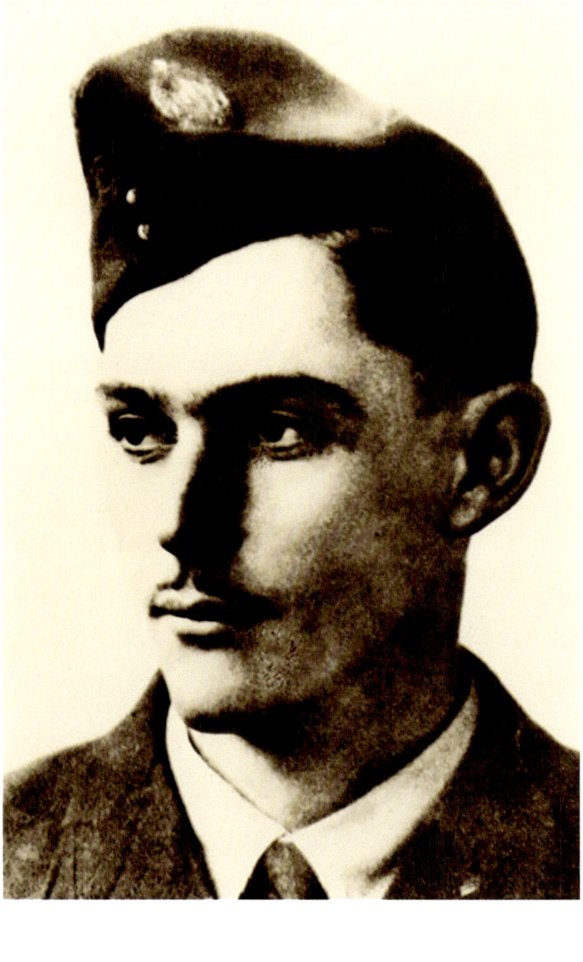

Rawdon Hume Middleton VC. (Australian War Memorial)

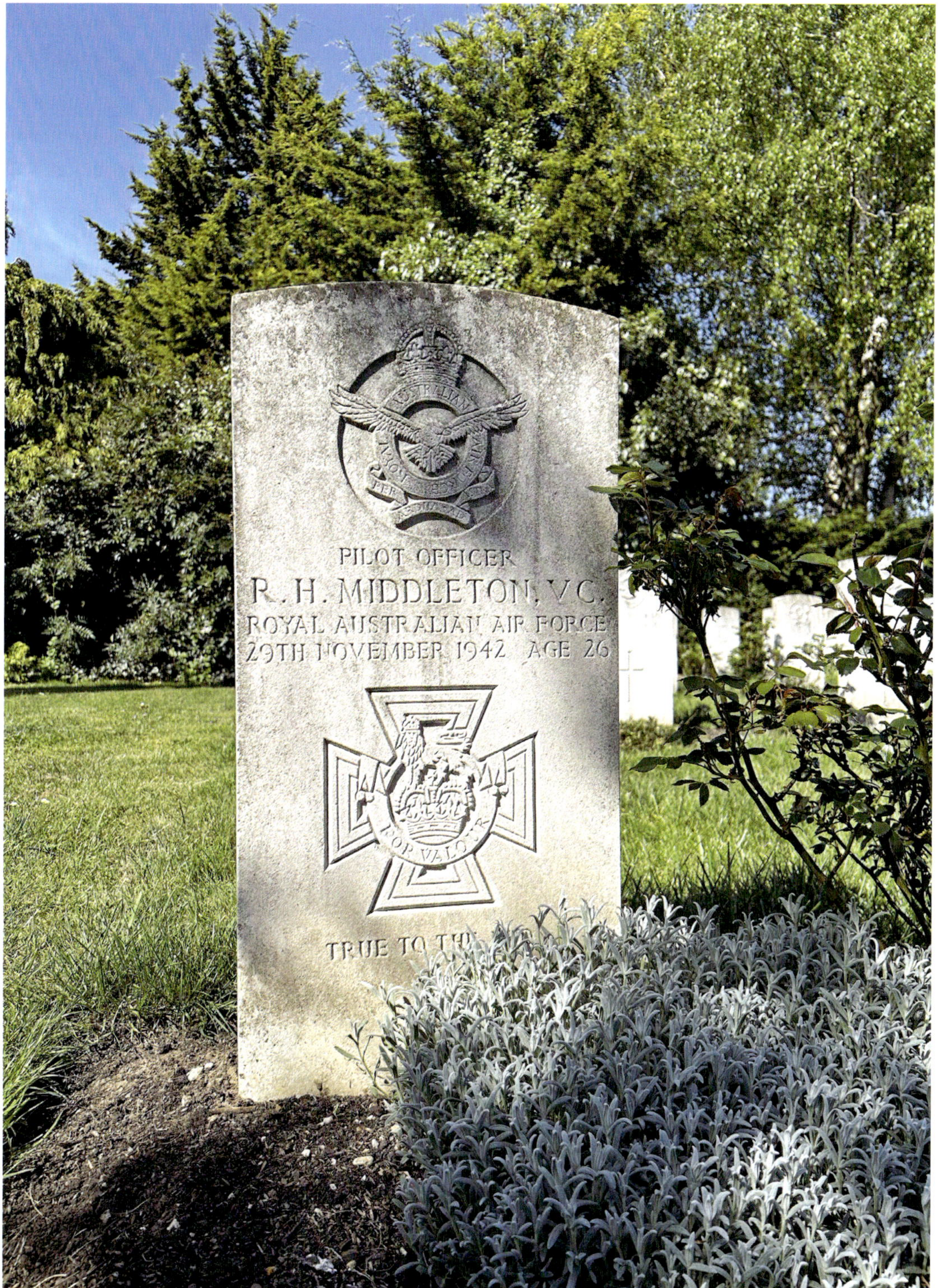

The grave of Rawden Hume Middleton VC at St John's churchyard, Beck Row.

1944. On 24 December 1944, Castle flew his thirtieth mission as co-pilot on the lead B-17, *Treble Four*, with the 487th Bomb Group, based at Lavenham airfield. Leading the air division of over 2,000 bombers to Liege, Belgium, Castle's aircraft lost one the engines en route, forcing the B-17 out of formation. The *Treble Four* was vulnerable to attacks from enemy fighters, which occurred almost immediately. Despite slowing them down, Castle refused to jettison his bombs knowing friendly troops were positioned below him. After repeated attacks and the loss of two more engines, Castle gave the order to bail-out. Castle remained at the bomber's controls, offering the opportunity for his crew to escape. Castle went down with his aircraft, but his sacrifice allowed five of the ten crew members to survive. Castle was posthumously awarded the United States' highest military award, the Congressional Medal of Honor, the highest-ranking member of the 8th USAAF to receive the decoration.

The Victoria Cross and Congressional Medal of Honor are the highest award for valour for their respective nations. Yet there are, however, many other individuals who were awarded medals for bravery which, although the incident didn't warrant the awarding of the VC or similar, are still more than worthy of mention. In 1941, Ambulance Driver Dorothy Clarke and Ambulance Attendant Bessie Jane Hepburn from Aldeburgh became the first women to be presented with the George Medal at Buckingham Palace. The George Medal was instituted in September 1940 as a decoration for acts of great bravery not in the presence of the enemy, that would not have been sufficient to warrant the award of

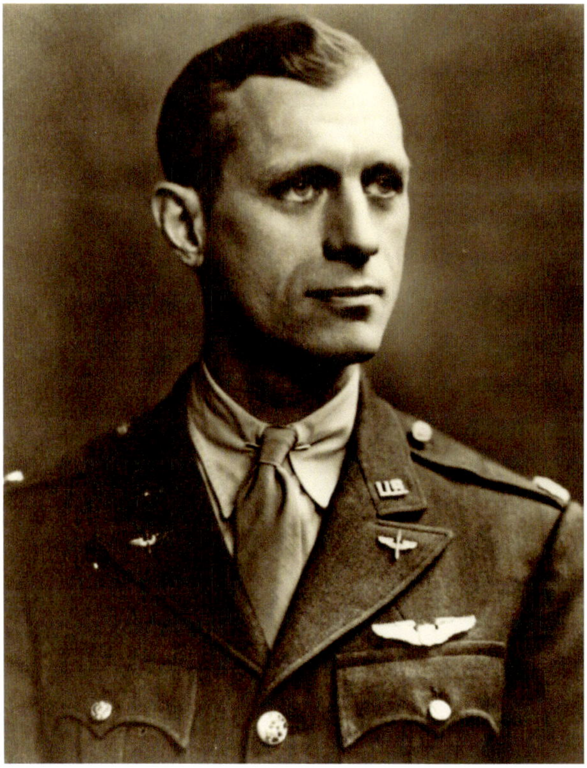

Brigadier General Frederick Castle, Medal of Honor. (United States Air Force Archive)

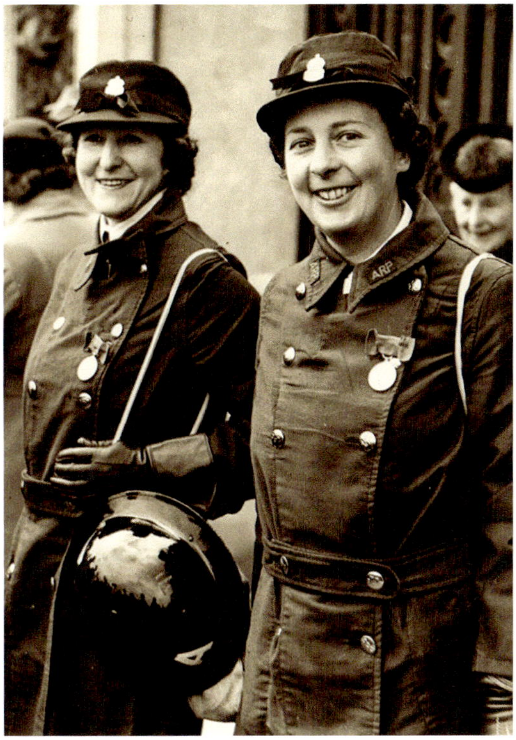

Ambulance Driver Dorothy Clarke (right) and Ambulance Attendant Bessie Jane Hepburn (left) after receiving their George Medal at Buckingham Palace in 1941. Clarke would be the first women to ever receive the medal, while Hepburn received her medal moments later. (Aldeburgh Museum Charitable Trust)

the George Cross (also instituted in 1940 for acts of gallantry not in the presence of the enemy, but equal in stature to the VC). In July 1940, Clarke and Hepburn responded to an incident at Aldeburgh where two soldiers had apparently entered a mined beach to go for a swim and had caused a mine to explode. In total disregard for their own safety, the pair of ambulance workers made their way onto the beach to recover the two soldiers. They found one man dead, and the other was seriously injured and would later die in hospital.

There are occasions where, despite their fascinating military career, it is for their deeds after a war which people are recognised. At the outbreak of the Second World War, Margaret Susan Ryder – better known as Sue Ryder – volunteered to serve in the First Aid Nursing Yeomanry, despite being underage (which seemed to go unnoticed by those who need know). Within a few years, she had been recruited for the secretive work of the Special Operations Executive (SOE). Working for the Polish Section of the SOE, Ryder assisted in the recruitment and training of Polish agents, who would be parachuted into Poland to coordinate resistance activities against the occupying German forces. Her admiration for the courageous men and women she helped prepare for the dangerous covert operations, and witnessing the devastation inflicted upon Warsaw and across the continent, led Ryder to decide to make it her life's mission to relieve the suffering of victims of the war. In 1953, she founded the charity named after herself, The Sue Ryder Foundation, at her mother's former home in Cavendish. Here, the charity provided concentration camp survivors with long-term nursing care, and in time grew to help others in need. In 1959, Sue Ryder married Group Captain Leonard Cheshire, a distinguished bomber pilot in the RAF. Cheshire received the VC in 1944, not for an individual act of valour, but for his bravery in the 100 missions he had flown over four years. Cheshire had himself set up similar homes and together the pair remained committed to their mission to help others. For her work, Ryder was appointed an Officer of the Order of the British Empire (OBE) in 1957, and a Companion of the Order of St Michael and St George (CMG) in 1976. In 1979, when Ryder was elevated to the House of Lords, her admiration for the people of Poland led her to taking the country's capital as part of her title – Lady Ryder of Warsaw. Ryder and Cheshire's final resting place is in the churchyard near the first Sue Ryder home in Cavendish.

There is no doubt that the examples of selfless courage above warrant the awards for gallantry the recipients duly received. However, there are many instances where personal bravery goes unnoticed, unrecorded and ultimately unrecognised. There are also occasions where specific acts of bravery of individuals are recorded and memorialised, but receive no further recognition. One such occasion occurred when British troops were sent to fight the Xhosa in the Eighth Cape Frontier Wars. In January 1852 a troopship, HMT *Birkenhead*, left Portsmouth with reinforcements for the British regiments already present in Cape Colony. In the early hours of 26 February 1852, the ship made its way round the Cape of Good Hope where it struck rocks off Danger Point and immediately began to take on water. As the soldiers, crew, women and children onboard assembled on deck, the order was given to lower the lifeboats for the women and children. Orders were given

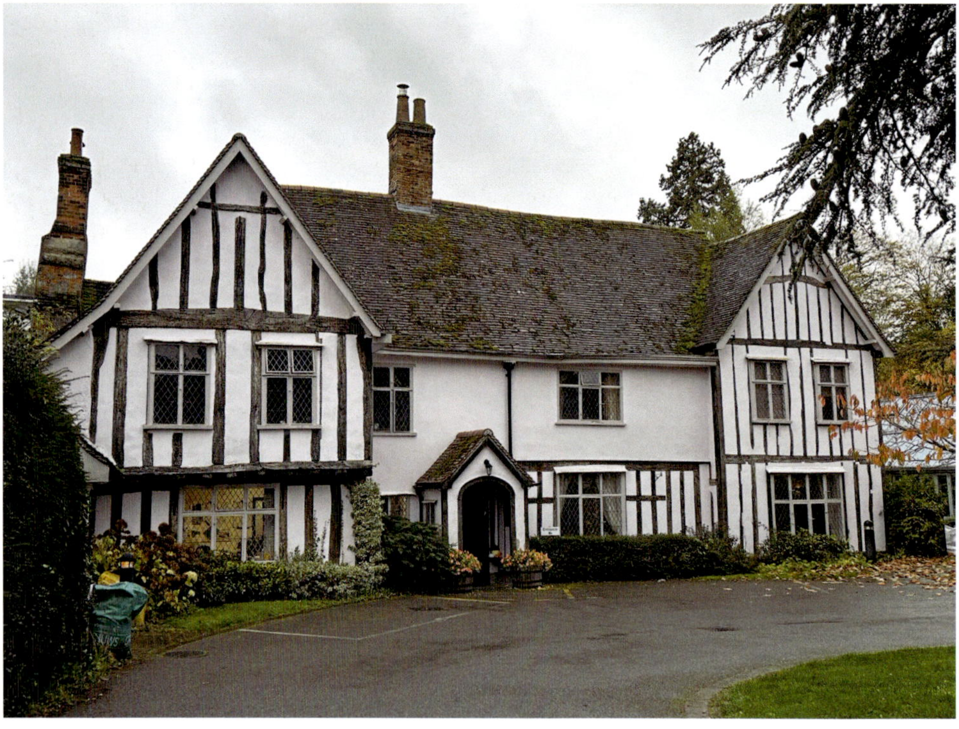

Ryder's family home in Cavendish would become the first Sue Ryder Foundation Home in 1953.

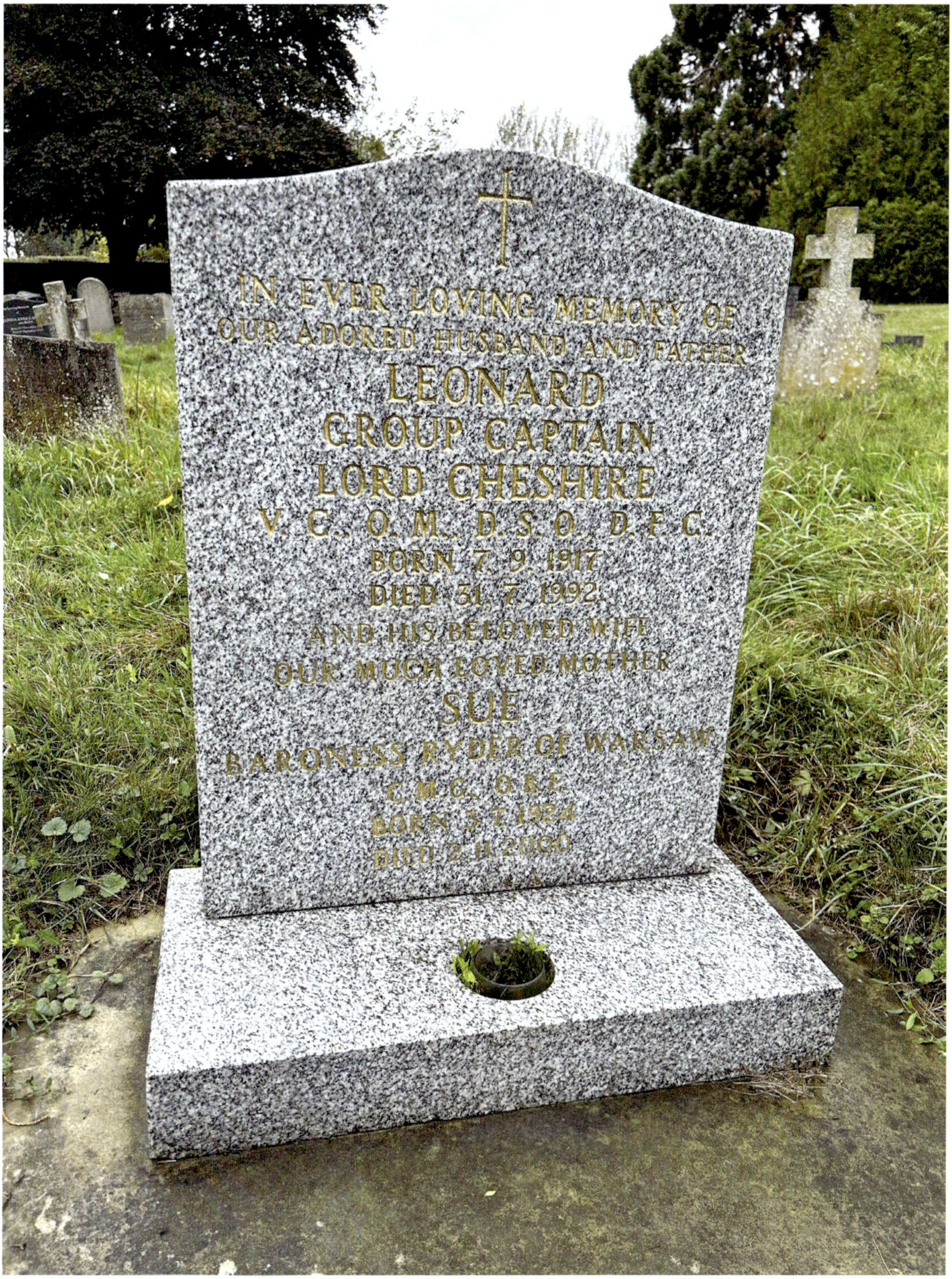

The grave of Leonard Cheshire VC at Cavendish's cemetery. Along with earning the VC, Cheshire also pioneered the new 'pathfinding' method, where low-flying aircraft dropped flares on targets to help the advancing bombers.

by the ship's commander for all those who could swim to jump overboard and head for the remaining lifeboats. Realising the danger this posed to the boats carrying the women and children, Colonel Seton of the 74th Regiment ordered the soldiers to 'stand fast', so the soldiers remained on deck in ranks as the ship broke apart. Among those 'standing fast' were fifty-five reinforcements for the 12th Regiment, all of whom succumbed to the shark-invested waters. The sinking of the *Birkenhead* gave rise to the 'Birkenhead Drill', more commonly known as 'women and children first' when abandoning a sinking ship. Although the discipline and selfless actions of the fifty-five men of the 12th no doubt helped save the lives of the women and children passengers, they received no honour or award for their bravery. However, the conduct of the officers and men onboard the Birkenhead did not go unnoticed, for the king of Prussia ordered that the 'magnificent behaviour of the troops' was to be recalled to the entire Prussian Army, while the General Officer Commanding the Forces in South Africa reported to the Duke of Wellington that 'true valour was never better exemplified'.

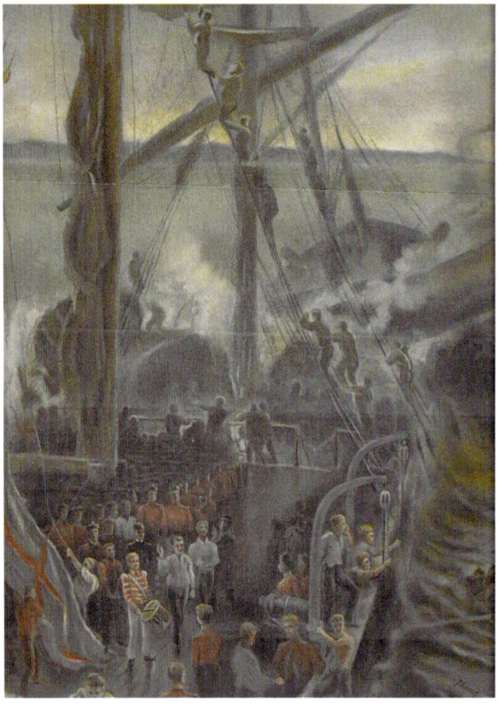

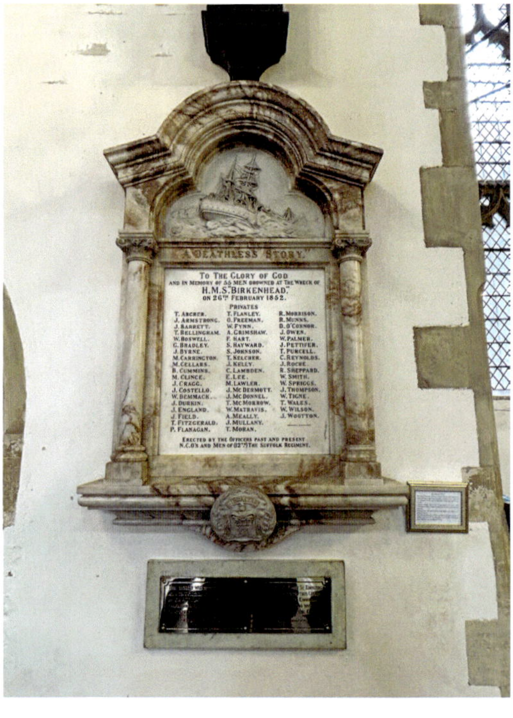

Above left: Print depicting the sinking of the *Birkenhead*.

Above right: Birkenhead memorial at St Mary's Church, Bury St Edmunds.

Suffolk Remembers

The most common physical reminder of military activity in any county in Britain is a war memorial, and Suffolk is no exception. It is safe to say that most people have walked or driven past one during their daily activities, whether known to them or not. In every town and almost every village you will find a memorial – often more than one – to those who fell in battle or as a direct result of war. These memorials take many forms and commemorate events from hundreds of years ago; the men and women who died in service with the army, navy or air force, and the civilians who died at home as the reach of warfare extended through the development of new technologies. The style and size of these memorials differ throughout the country, and this is mirrored at the county level. From impressive public works and curious monuments to simple and modest acknowledgements of sacrifice, these touching reminders of the local area's military contribution are sometimes blurred into the urban background.

The style and size of war memorials varies between the different towns and villages across Suffolk, and their construction is often rooted in the designs of earlier memorials. The revival of earlier memorial designs, such as the use of obelisks, originates from British victories over the French in Egypt during late eighteenth and early nineteenth centuries; the use of columns in commemorating military events dates from antiquity. Monumental crosses that were erected by the early Christian church were adopted by the Crusaders and became martially linked, which was strengthened by the cruciform shape of the sword. While specific designs for memorials demonstrate the styles and philosophies of client and sculptor, the three most common features of war memorials are the cross, obelisk and column, and they often combine more than one of these features.

While the end of the First World War marked the start of a great period of memorial construction, there are many memorials from earlier conflicts in numerous locations across Suffolk, including that of the 'gallant and courageous' Lieutenant Colonel Collier of the Coldstream Guards. Collier was with the Guards for fourteen years, where his service took him to Egypt, Germany, Denmark, Portugal, Spain and eventually France, where on 10 May 1814 he would die from the severe wounds he received during the attack on the French at Bayonne. A memorial plaque to Lieutenant Colonel Collier can be found in St Mary's Church at Bury St Edmunds. Charles Hill of Buxhall served during the New Zealand War onboard the unarmoured wooden corvette HMS *Orpheus*, between 1861 and 1863. On 7 February 1863, the *Orpheus* was wrecked along the west coast of New Zealand on the bar of Manukau Harbour, with the loss of 189 of her crew. The sandbanks near the mouth of the harbour had moved since the Admiralty chart was completed in 1853, and although this information was included in the *Orpheus's* charts, it appears those on the bridge took little notice. Lieutenant Hill was one of eight officers who survived the wreck. This incident was an ominous sign for Hill's time in New Zealand; while serving

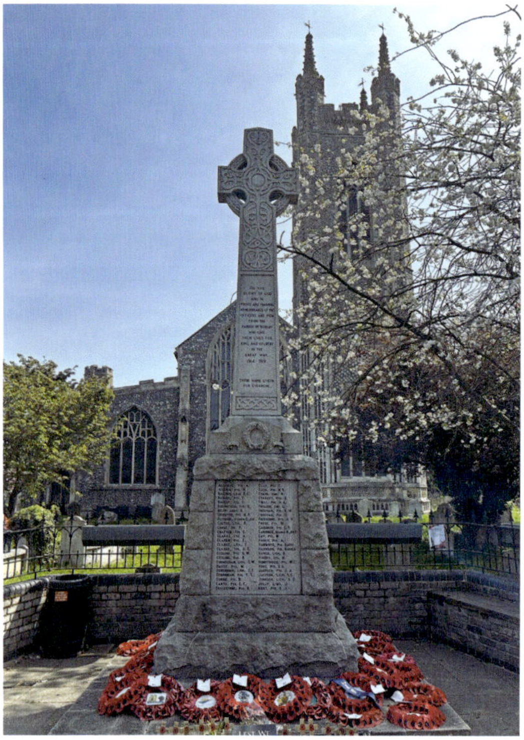

Bungay's War Memorial uses the Celtic cross.

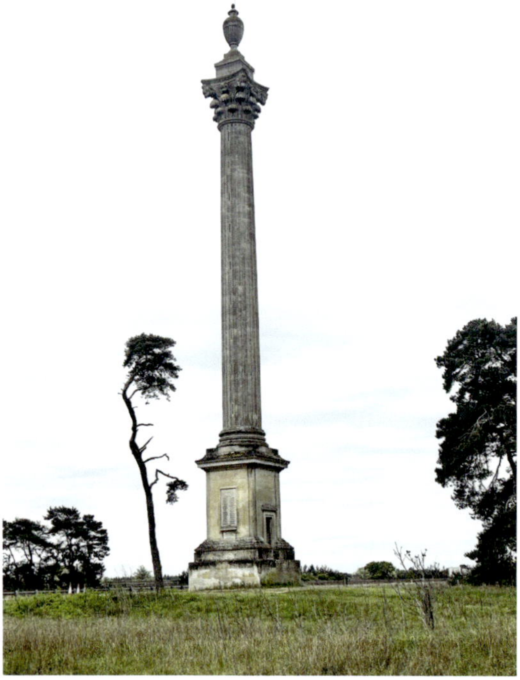

The Elveden Memorial. The column stands over 30 metres tall, at the boundaries of the three parishes on the Elvedon Estate (Elveden, Eriswell and Iclingham), whose fallen it commemorates.

on HMS *Curacoa*, Hill was killed by a gunshot wound to his right cheek and upper part of the sternum on 29 April 1864 during the Battle of Gate Pa. Erected by his messmates, a brass tablet commemorates his death in the village church at Buxhall. The Boer War of 1899–1902 marked the first period of extensive memorial building across the country. Albert Toft, who had apprenticed at the Wedgwood factories and later studied sculpture at the Royal College of Art, was commissioned to create several Boer War memorials, including the one at Ipswich. Toft's sculpture introduces the anonymous soldier as a hero, mourning with his head bowed and holding his rifle with the muzzle resting on his left boot. The soldier became a symbolic figure: by mourning the ordinary heroic soldier, their comrades who mourn are themselves, by extension, equally heroic.

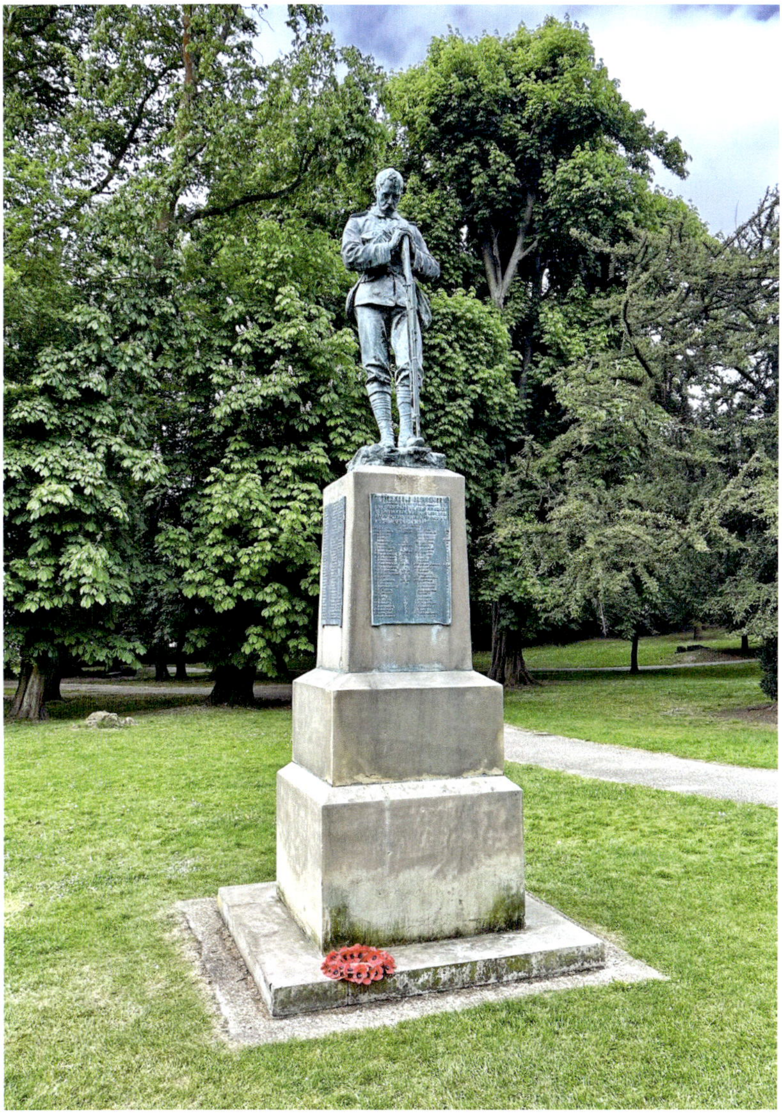

Boer War Memorial designed by Toft at Christchurch Park, Ipswich.

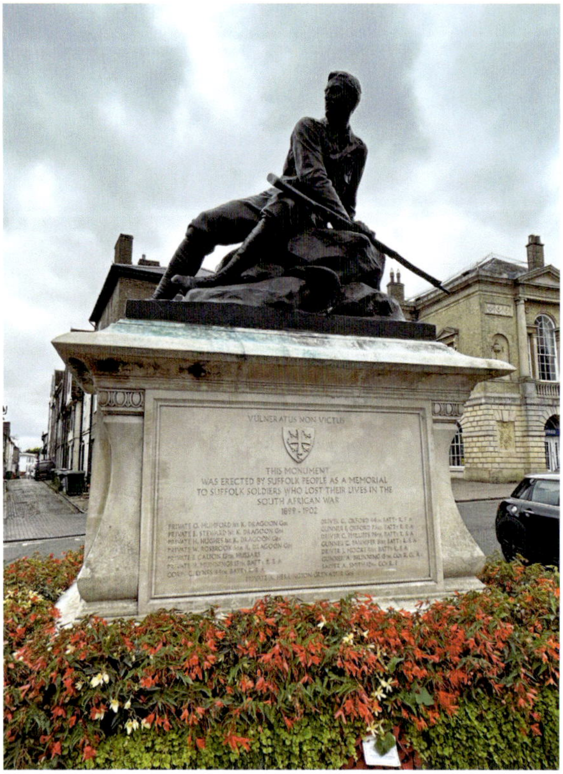

Boer War Memorial at Market Square, Bury St Edmunds. The ordinary solider became the inspiration behind many Boer War memorials across the country.

The end of the First World War marked the beginning of widespread memorial construction across entire country. It soon became clear to the military and civilian authorities that the repatriation of those who had died in service was an impossible task. Memorials would become a place where those who lost sons, fathers and husbands could come to remember, commemorate their sacrifice and find or offer support to those grieving. As memorials in towns and villages were built across the county, the names on these memorials could often be found on additional memorials, such those who attended a specific church or school, local employers and private memorials. Edward Lake, the Managing Director of the Greene King brewery at Bury St Edmunds, funded the Victory Sports Ground and Pavilion to give thanks to those employees who survived their military service, and to remember those employees who did not return. In addition to the more common style of memorials – such as the winged angel representing 'Victory', Celtic and Christian crosses, columns, and modest brass plaques – there are an abundance of different ways that military service has been memorialised, such as memorial halls, hospitals, and homes. Stained-glass windows are another style of memorial found in churches throughout Suffolk. Lieutenant Colonel Charles Hotham Montagu Dougherty-Wylie of Theberton Hall, attached to the HQ Mediterranean Expeditionary Force from the Royal Welsh Fusiliers, led an assault on Hill 141 behind the old fort of Sedd-el-Bahr, Gallipoli, on 26 April 1915. Despite the enemy's entrenched position, defended by concealed machine guns, the attack was successful. As a result, the landing area of 'V Beach' was now secure. However, Doughtery-Wylie was killed in the moment of victory and was posthumously awarded the Victoria Cross. In St Peter's Church near his home in Theberton, a stained-glass window commemorates his life and service. Wylie is portrayed as St George, dressed in medieval armour and holding a sword, a slain dragon by his feet, as he kneels before a cross at the summit of the hill. The Victoria Cross recipient Skipper Thomas Crisp, whose heroism is recounted in chapter five, has the unusual distinction of having a church bell dedicated to his memory. In the ringer's room on the ground floor of St Margaret's Church, Lowestoft, a brass plaques recalls to whom the eight bells are engraved. Bell number 7 (tuned to G sharp) is dedicated to Crisp.

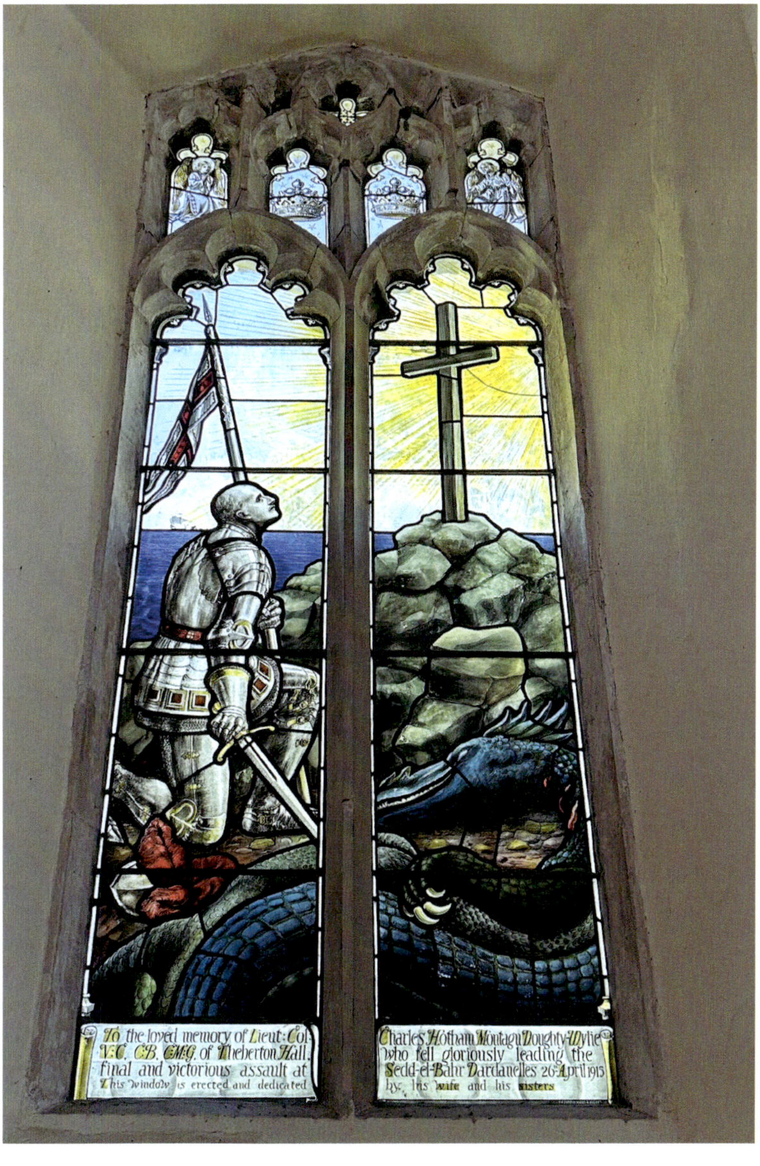

The elaborate stained-glass memorial to Lieutenant Colonel Charles Hotham Montagu Dougherty-Wylie at St Peter's Church, Theberton.

It can be said with a degree of certainty that the First World War had an impact on every village and town in Suffolk, whether because of the actions of those serving their country or the affect this had on those at home. However, not every village has a war memorial dedicated to those who lost their lives serving king and country, simply because there are a rare few that can consider themselves a 'thankful village'. On the east wall of the St Botolph's Church, Culpho, is a memorial made from an arrangement of glass tiles. It is not a memorial for those from the village who fell, as there were none, but rather a sign of 'thankfulness' that the war was over. The term a 'thankful village' is credited to British writer Arthur Mee in his counties guide *The King's England* and describes those villages who had all those who served return home. The second of only two villages in Suffolk noted to be a 'thankful village' is St Michael South Elmham. Indeed, St Michael South Elmham has the very rare distinction of being 'doubly thankful', because the eleven men who served in the First World War and the seven men and women who served during the Second World War all returned home. Though it is important to remember that for those who served and returned, they no doubt bore the physical and mental scars from their service.

There have been fewer memorials constructed post-1945, partly due to the number of First World War memorials that had only been completed just before the outbreak of war in 1939. There are of course many exceptions to this; those familiar with former RAF and USAAF airfields will often find memorials dedicated to those who left the runways and would never return home. Given the vast Suffolk coastline and the training and headquarters of naval forces that operated from there, as well as the number of naval vessels that patrolled the waters, it is no surprise that the memorials to those who lost their lives at sea during the two world wars can be found in coastal towns. Such memorials include the Merchant Navy memorial at Ipswich's Waterfront, Orwell Quay, and the Lowestoft Naval Memorial in Belle Vue Park which commemorates 2,399 sailors of the Royal Naval Patrol Service who have no grave but the sea.

The memorials constructed to remember those who died in the First World War would later be adapted to include the names of those who died in the Second World War, and also more recent conflicts. In the town of Hadleigh, the Cenotaph War Memorial was unveiled in June 1921 to 'perpetuate the memory of those who had fallen' during the First World War; it now includes the names of those who died during the Second World War on a wall behind the existing First World War memorial, while a separate memorial marks the passing of Staff Sergeant Sharron Elliott. In 2006 she had been deployed to Iraq to fill a temporary post but had volunteered to stay for the remainder of the six-month tour. Elliott was killed on Remembrance Sunday while on a routine boat patrol. Elliott's Rigid Raiding Craft was hit by an IED mounted on a bridge on the Shatt Al Arab River on the eastern edge of Basra city. Elliot was the first female soldier to be killed in action in Iraq, but sadly not the last. An even more recent memorial to the Suffolk's military sacrifice is that commemorating the death of Lance Corporal of Horse Jonathon Woodgate of the Household Cavalry (Blues & Royals). On 26 March 2010, on his second tour of Afghanistan, Corporal Woodgate was walking towards the helicopter that would take him away from his final patrol of the tour when his group came under small arms fire, east of Sangin. Woodgate was killed from an explosion from and enemy grenade, aged twenty-six. His

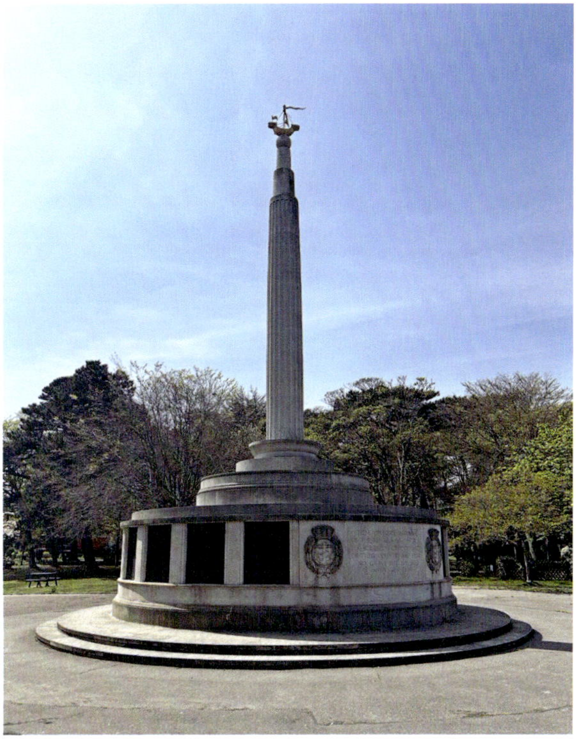

Rght: The Royal Naval Patrol Service Memorial at Belle Vue Park, Lowestoft.

Below: Lowestoft became the Central Depot for the RNPS during the Second World War, with its headquarters, HMS Europa (often referred to as the 'Sparrows Nest'), located in the Municipal Gardens.

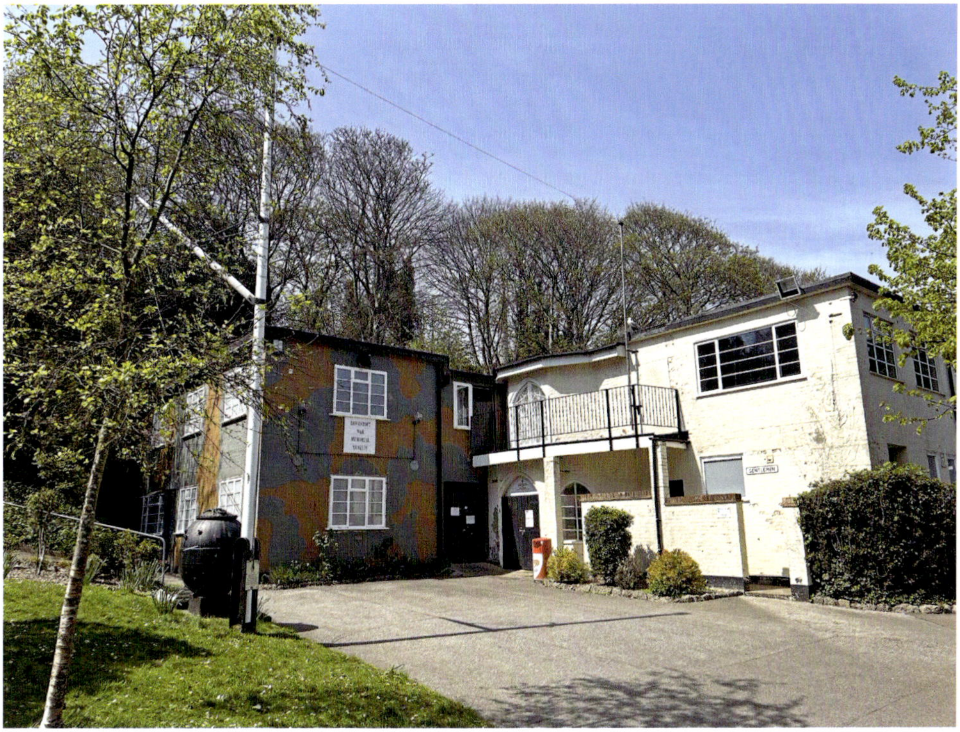

service and sacrifice are remembered in Suffolk by a modest plaque located on the wall adjacent to the Guildhall in Lavenham's Market Square, where he spent over half of his life, and in All Saints Church in the village of Chelsworth, where he was born and is now buried.

There is no more poignant reminder of military service than the final resting place for those who made the ultimate sacrifice. Commonwealth War Graves Commission headstones can be found in church cemeteries across the county. While these are usually few in number and nestled in between civilian headstones dating back centuries, in Ipswich, Lowestoft, and Shotley, the rows of distinctive Portland limestone headstones offer a sobering glimpse of the sheer scale of human loss caused by both world wars. These cemeteries in Suffolk are also a microcosm of the global scale of the wars, where casualties from the Netherlands Merchant Navy, Polish Army, Royal Australian Air Force, Royal New Zealand Air Force, and Royal Canadian Air Force are buried alongside both their British Army allies and those they fought against. While the subtle and dignified appearance of the CWGC headstone has a timeless quality to its design, and many other traditional memorials pay homage to the past with their architectural features, a more contemporary memorial design can be found in Abbey Gardens in Bury St Edmunds. In January 2015, a polished stainless-steel teardrop-shaped sculpture was placed in a small garden area to remember all victims of genocide. Yet this is not the only way victims

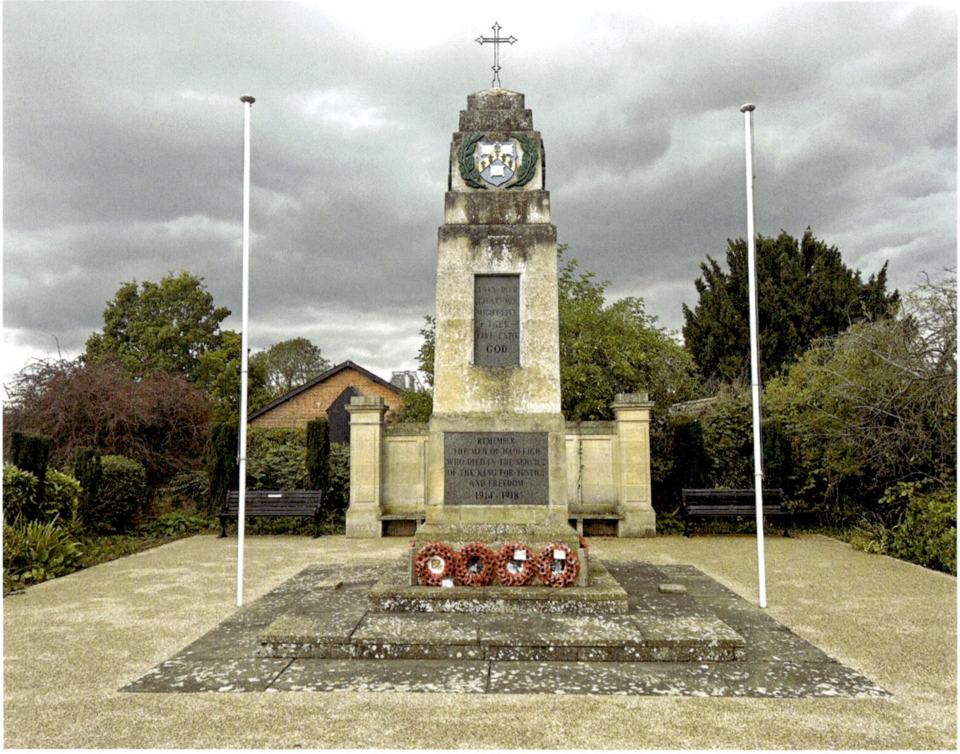

Hadleigh's Cenotaph War Memorial.

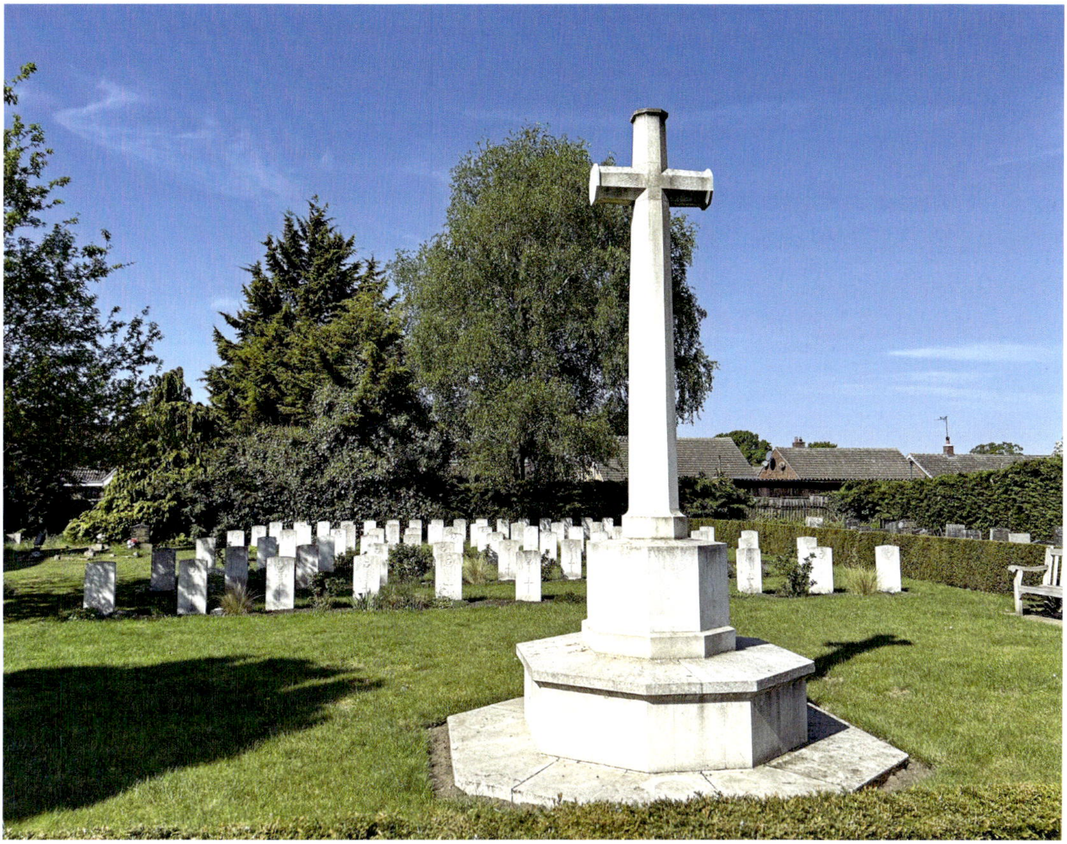

Rows of Commonwealth War Grave Commission headstones at Beck Row, including RAF, Royal New Zealand Air Force, Royal Australian Air Force, and 'Unknown Airmen' who flew from nearby RAF Mildenhall during the Second World War.

and survivors of holocausts are remembered in Suffolk. As mentioned in the previous chapter, the final resting place of Group Captain Leonard Cheshire VC and Sue Baroness Ryder of Warsaw is Cavendish Cemetery, near their family home that would become the first Sue Ryder Care Home. Ryder's wartime and post-war service in Poland resulted in Jewish-Polish survivors of Nazi concentration camps making Cavendish their home. These survivors would live the remainder of their lives in the peace and tranquillity of this idyllic Suffolk village and are laid to rest next to Cheshire and Ryder.

This chapter is a fitting way to end this book on Suffolk's Military Heritage. While the surviving structures in Suffolk's landscape may pique the interest of many who wish to learn more about their construction and purpose, it is paramount when exploring the subject of war to remember the suffering and destruction caused by these events.

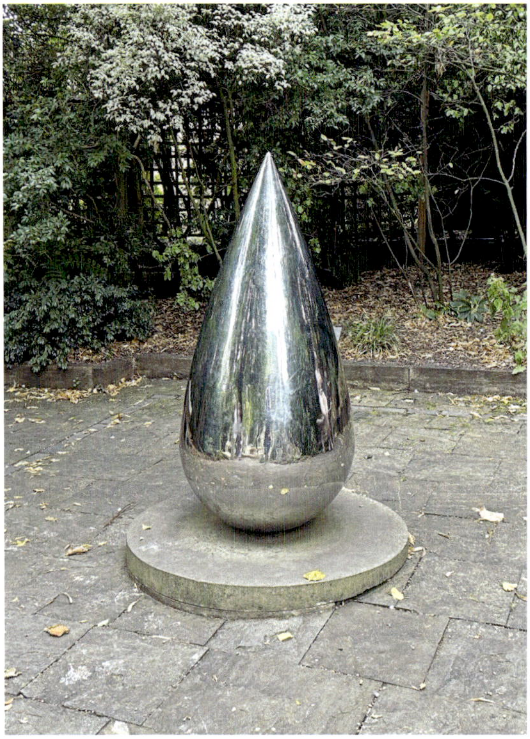

The 'Teardrop' memorial to all victims of genocide in Abbey Gardens, Bury St Edmunds.

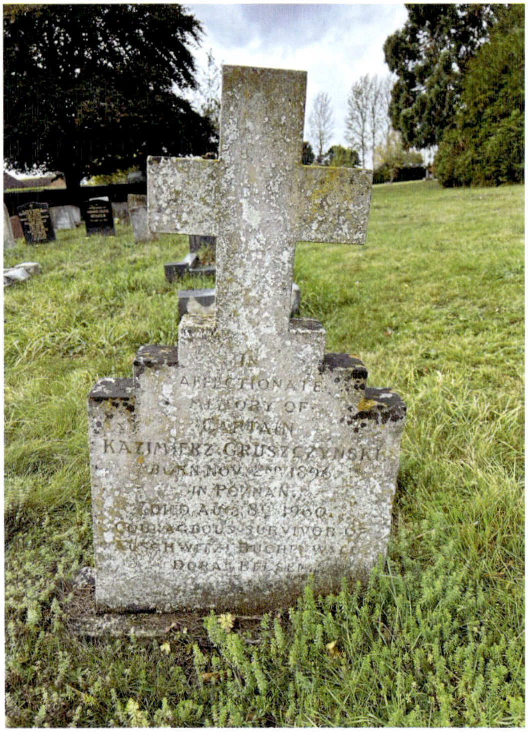

Holocaust survivor Kazimierz Gruszczynski, buried at Cavendish Cemetery. An officer serving in the Polish Army at the outbreak of the Second World War, he joined the Polish Underground in January 1941, working against the German occupation of Poland until he was arrested for the final time in April 1943. He remained a prisoner at Nazi concentration camps until April 1945.

Acknowledgements

I would like to acknowledge the numerous sources for the stories I have explored, and more importantly thank the many individuals and institutions who provided information and allowed the reproduction of images; their help has been invaluable in completing this publication.

For their assistance in aiding my research I would like to thank the staff and volunteers at the Suffolk Archives, Suffolk Libraries, and the county's countless museums and heritage centres. I would also like to offer my thanks to Tamsin Appell of Bachelors Hall for kindly allowing me to photograph her family home and using the image in this book. For use of images, I am grateful to: Aldeburgh Museum Charitable Trust, National Archives, D.C., United States Air Force Archive, Naval History and Heritage Command, and the Australian War Memorial.

Finally, I would like to thank Amberley Publishing for allowing me the opportunity to write this book, and my wife, Angela, and daughter, Willa, for their unwavering support and assistance.

About the Author

Adam Culling is a historian and former museum curator who has had a lifetime interest in military history. Adam is an Associate Fellow of the Royal Historical Society. He is the author of *Essex's Military Heritage* and editor of the books *Fighting Fit 1914* and *Fighting Fit 1939*. He lives on the Essex/Suffolk border with his wife and daughter.